To:
Sean
God Bless!

Living it Loud
Bandimere
SUPER CHARGED

FAITH, FAMILY &
the PURSUIT OF SPEED

by
CHAD BONHAM

Forewords by John Force and Don Garlits

CONTENTS

Dedication

This book is lovingly dedicated first to the Lord Jesus Christ who first loved us, gave His life for us, and by faith accepted us into His family through a personal relationship.

Secondly we dedicate this book to our Mom, Frances Victoria Bandimere, who not only knew how to express God's love to all she met and touched, but who supported and inspired our Dad, John Bandimere Sr., in ways that were exactly what he needed from a life partner. She exemplified and was a powerful example of a wife who understood how to love her man in a true covenant way.

There are individuals who have been a part of our lives from day one. These are amazingly wonderful people willing to be employees of the various businesses we were privileged to operate. Their dedication, talent and commitment will forever be appreciated and never forgotten. If this book gets into your hands, we would love to have you send us an "update" about you and your family.

And to our customers, how does one express adequate thanks for the support and encouragement from those who shared our love of cars and performance.

Where would we be without the Lord, a godly Mom and Dad, and all of our family members, wonderful employees, customers and friends?

Heartfelt thanks to all... – *The Bandimere Family*

Acknowledgements

First and foremost, I want to thank God for blessing me with the opportunity to share inspirational stories with others through the written word. I strive to never take for granted the privilege of the author's platform.

Next, I need to thank my gracious wife Amy for her patience and steadfast support. As I was wrapping up work on this book, we were facing some incredible challenges and she held down the fort and took care of so many things that I could not. I also want to acknowledge the inspiration I get from my incredible sons Lance, Cole and Quinn. They daily fuel my fire.

Of course, this project wouldn't have been possible without the support and input from the entire Bandimere family. Thank you John Bandimere Jr. and Tami Shrader (Bandimere) for spearheading this project and to David Bandimere and his son Skip Bandimere for providing so much vital historical information. Thanks also to Lorraine Bandimere, Barbara Bandimere, Rich and Joanna Gager, Larry and Johnna Crispe, John III (Sporty) and Debbie Bandimere, Randy Gager, Rick Gager, Russ Gager and Susan Brown.

This book also wouldn't have happened had Lisa Edwards not first put me in touch with the Bandimere family. Her foresight was a huge reason behind my participation. Thanks also go to Gordon Thiessen who continues to provide me with incredible opportunities to publish great stories through Cross Training Publishing and exhibits uncommon patience every step of the way. I also want to acknowledge the graphic designers at U.S. Recognition for doing such a fantastic job creating the concept for the book's cover art.

Finally, special thanks go out to the many individuals who contributed to this book through commentaries, stories and invaluable insights: George Abbas, John Abbott, Bill Armstrong, Bob Brockmeyer, Antron Brown, Steve Ciancio, Mike Edwards, John Force, Dallas Gardner, Don Garlits, Jim Groen, Roger Guzman, Bob Harmsen, Jim Head, Joe Hilger, Eddie Hill, Dave Howery, Dave Jackson, Bob Janowski, Allen Johnson, Rob Johnson, Ron Leslie, Harry Lindsay, Dave McClelland, Wayne McMurtry, Doug Miller, Mitch Mustard, Ron Neff, Rod Olson, Rob Park, Allan Perotin,

Butch Salter, Larry Smiley, Bruce Tawson, Jim Taylor, Tim Travis, Mark Williams and Darrell Zimmerman.

On a special note, I want to make sure to mention the contribution of Dr. David Beckman who went to be with Jesus just six weeks after I was fortunate to meet with him and his daughter Andrea Stark. It was an incredible blessing to spend time with Dr. Beckman along with some members of the Bandimere family and hear about his divine intersection with John Bandimere Sr.

And finally, I trust that everyone who reads this book will gain a greater understanding of what it looks like when a family follows the Father's plan and trusts Him no matter challenges may come their way. May God richly bless you all. – *Chad Bonham*

Foreword by John Force

It was 1979 when I first came to Denver and experienced the beauty of Bandimere Speedway carved in that mountain. I believe God carved it there. I really do. It is the most beautiful racetrack on the circuit. I'm not saying it's the biggest track with the most colossal stadium. But it's like a poster–something majestic. You don't see something like that very often and I hope it never goes away.

Up until my first visit there, I had hardly left California. So when I came over the pass, I saw a snow-covered city and had no idea how I was going to get back home. In those days, a lot of track operators wouldn't pay you if you didn't run. I just knew my match race was going to get cancelled and I was going to get stranded in Denver.

What I found instead was a very honorable family. I was a big nobody, but if something would have happened and we didn't get to run the race, they weren't going to let me starve to death. They were going to figure out a way to get me home. Somehow we managed to race that weekend and the family took very good care of me. That's the kind of people they were back then and that's the kind of people they still are today.

Even with all of its beauty, it's the Bandimere family that makes Bandimere Speedway special. I'm a fan of John Bandimere Jr. He has grown the sport of drag racing. He's also a man of his word and he's been there for me in some very dark times.

As you read this book, I hope you enjoy the stories about John Bandimere Sr., and how the track was built, how it has grown, and how it has survived in the face of some incredible challenges. But most importantly, I hope you see a family with strong convictions that stands by their faith in God when times are good and when times are bad. – *John Force*

Foreword by Don Garlits

When I first arrived at Bandimere Speedway, it was because the family had hired me to compete in a match race against John Abbott. I was immediately amazed at the site of a drag strip carved out of the side of that mountain. I couldn't imagine the extreme trouble that John Bandimere Sr. and his family went through to build a track in such a beautiful location.

One of my best memories of the track was also one my scariest moments. It was July of 1986, just a week after I had experienced a spectacular wheel stand in my Swamp Rat XXX in Englishtown, New Jersey. For the Mopar Parts Mile-High NHRA Nationals, I put wheelie bars on the car to prevent another such happening.

Wouldn't you know, the parachute got entangled in the contraption, and I had to stop without the aid of that vital piece of safety equipment. At the time, there was a small cliff at the very end of the strip and my front wheels were hanging over the edge when I stopped. I didn't run with those bars ever again!

But my fondest memories in Denver have been the times I've spent around so many good people. The Bandimere family has always done what they said they would do and their Christian faith has made our friendship even better.

I hope that you enjoy reading about the excitement of drag racing at over 5,000 feet above sea level. And maybe someone will be brought into a relationship with Christ. Even if just one person, the effort to put this book together would have been worth it.

– *Don Garlits*

Introduction

"For it is by grace you have been saved, through faith–and this is not from yourselves, it is the gift of God– not by works, so that no one can boast." Ephesians 2:8-9 (NIV)

After 55 years of operating a racetrack in the beautiful Colorado foothills, one can only imagine the stories that need to be told. That's why this book was written–to capture some of the history of the Bandimere Family. Many times, I have shared stories of the past to my immediate family around the dinner table as well as to our racing family over the public address system during a race about the things my father had done or accomplished in his life.

Each time a story was told, it was followed by comments not only of appreciation for sharing a piece of our family's history, but also with requests for more stories and the suggestion of documenting these memories so they can be enjoyed for years to come. It is impossible to be in the automotive business for over 60 years and the racing industry for over 55 years without having plenty of experiences and it is amazing how many of our friends remember specific circumstances or incidents better than me!

Very few members of our racing family are unaware of our family's love for God and the thankfulness we have for the grace, mercy and love that He has shown us. Being a family that works together on a daily basis is not as easy as one might think. In fact, I hope that this book will be one of encouragement to all of the readers, as well as to my family, as we all are reminded of God's favor in our lives.

Are we special? Absolutely not! We are sinners saved by grace. Do we struggle with each other? Yes we do–just like any other family that is together 24/7.

Do we want to quit at times and not spend every weekend of the summer tied down to operating events, dealing with weather conditions, early mornings and late nights? Of course those thoughts go through our minds.

But when you have grown up without the word "quit" in your vocabulary, we continue on and find that we have been blessed beyond measure by so many people that we can truly say have become friends and extended family to us.

When my family seriously suggested that it was time to stop talking about putting all our stories into a book and just do it, I knew that we needed to find an author who could tell our story in a way that would not only give a picture of our family's successes and shortcomings, but also understand how important it was to show that without the Lord's continuous leading throughout the years, anything we have accomplished would be empty.

Through our good friend Lisa Edwards, we were introduced to Chad Bonham who enthusiastically agreed to give our project a shot and has no doubt learned more about the automotive and racing industry than he ever wanted to know. Through trips from his home in Oklahoma to Colorado, Chad has patiently listened, recorded, written, typed, edited, and demonstrated a tremendous amount of grace for the task we set before him. I'm sure we have found a new drag racing fan through all this!

My mom Frances, who passed way too early in life at the age of 53, has this inscription on her tombstone: "She speaks to you . . . Do you know my Jesus?"

A life without Christ is like a drag car without an engine. It has no power! My personal prayer for those who take the time to read this book would be that they ask themselves, "When I die, am I sure I am going to Heaven?"

Blessings to you as you spend time enjoying the stories shared by many in this book. Know that you are loved. —*John C. Bandimere Jr.*

1

A Day
On Thunder Mountain

It's a mild Friday morning in Morrison, Colorado. That will change soon enough. Late afternoon temperatures in late July typically get close to 90 degrees. And that's not taking in account the extra heat that over 400 race cars generate as the engines burn up either Nitromethane or racing fuel.

As John Bandimere Jr. drives down West Alameda Avenue towards Rooney Road, he has already had a busy week. Preparing for the annual Mopar Mile-High NHRA Nationals is unlike any other time of the year. A few days, earlier, his staff made sure that the nearly 400 staff members had received their uniforms, credentials and parking passes.

On Wednesday, the sponsors and professional race teams arrived at the track and jockeyed for the most desired parking spots. Bandimere Speedway isn't known for having vast amounts of space and it never ceases to amaze Bandimere Jr. how so many semi-trailers and so much support equipment can park so closely together without touching.

Thursday was particularly hectic with a golf tournament in the morning that benefitted the Bandimere family's Race To Read® program, a press conference downtown, and that evening's Mopar Golden Street Party on Washington Street in downtown Golden that featured food, live music, autograph sessions, a car show and bench racing for thousands of fans to enjoy. Back at the track during the morning and afternoon, race teams continued to arrive and go through the tedious tech inspection process.

Even today, after decades of pulling through the gate, it never fails that Bandimere Jr. has to catch his breath as the site of the race-track nestled beside the mountainside reveals itself. For the time being, Bandimere Speedway is relatively quiet and calm–that is if you can ignore the bustling activity that envelops every inch of the facility.

Race teams have completed registration. The Safety Safari has set up their compound at the top end of the track with their trucks, four-wheelers and safety equipment from their haulers. The NHRA souvenir trailers are in position and merchandisers are ready to sell their T-shirts and novelty items. Packages for the race teams are being picked up at the postal trailer that has been arranged to receive and distribute mail throughout the long weekend. Tents are visible everywhere. Tables and chairs have been set up and arranged for hospitality over the weekend. Food vendors are hunkered down in their designated areas and prepared to feed an average of 30,000 plus fans daily over the next three days. ESPN has been laying down cable, mounting cameras and setting up its broadcast truck, ready to record the day's race event.

Bandimere Jr. sits at his desk in an adjacent building on the east-side of the track. He calls a radio station or two for quick on-air interviews to promote the event. His desk houses a stack of books that espouse the value of biblical leadership. Bandimere Jr. is sober-ly aware of the fact that the principles learned from his daily read-ing habit and his years of experience will be tested as soon as he steps out of his office and into the demanding drag racing world. So he gathers himself for that one last bit of peace he will need to sus-tain him through Sunday.

It wasn't that long ago when the entire event weighed heavily on his shoulders. In the earliest days of the national event, he would have a recurring dream of opening the gates for the race but no one had shown up. Bandimere Jr. hasn't harbored that fear for a while now. It has been replaced with excitement and anticipation. He looks forward to seeing lots of trash on the ground because lots of trash means lots of people were there. Even more so, he eagerly awaits the opportunity to converse with good friends that he hasn't seen since the year before.

As he grabs his earplugs and heads to the command center in the speedway's tower, Bandimere Jr. knows better than most how much of a miracle it is that this day is actually taking place. He along with his older sister Joanna Gager and his younger brother David Bandimere are well aware of the dubious life circumstances that could have snuffed out his father's dream 25 years before it was even conceived. He is also intimately familiar with more recent events that threatened to bring the family's amazing journey to an end.

But here Bandimere Jr. stands, looking across a race facility appropriately dubbed "Thunder Mountain" that strangely looks as natural as the hogback that sits to its immediate west. He's been known to refer to it as "God's handiwork" and he never tires of the view.

He also has no choice but to acknowledge the divine process that led to this very moment in time.

2

Sowing the
Seeds of Speed

John Bandimere Sr. never liked farming. But there he was on a farm thinking up excuses within his creative young mind to do anything *but* farm. His favorite activity was taking apart farm equipment and teaching himself the inner workings of the engine. There was only one problem. Sometimes he didn't know how to put them back together.

Not surprisingly, this usually upset his father Fred Bandimere who was noted for his fastidious nature. He was also very organized. His son was not. Much to Fred Bandimere's chagrin, various car and engine parts and random tools were often left strewn across the front lawn of the farmhouse.

For one of his early projects, Bandimere Sr. tore down a tractor and put Buick pistons with higher compression in the engine to make it go faster. Not exactly a necessary trait for the average commercial vehicle, but rather something sure fired to incur his father's ire.

Bandimere Sr. didn't know it yet, but he was experiencing the pull of God's calling in life. He had a natural affinity for mechanics and in particular automotive performance. Although he felt out of place at the moment, Bandimere Sr. was walking out a journey that preceded him many years into the past and required providential interventions along the way.

Coming To America

In the late 1840s and early 1850s, there was a significant exodus from Germany that included many of the nation's Prussian population. For some, it was a chance to escape a suppression of the patch-work country's so-called "liberals" or "48ers" that had pushed through the first half of the 19th Century for a unified Germany. It also provided an opportunity to seek out greater economic freedom abroad.

Such was the case for a 49-year old man from Neu Paleshken, West Prussia, named Johann Bandemer who traveled to the United States in 1853 with his 12 children and a nanny. Bandemer arrived in the Port of New Orleans where the family members received English spellings for their names. Bandemer was still grieving the loss of his wife who had tragically died not long prior to their departure.

After landing at the Port of New Orleans, the large group traveled north along the Mississippi River. Due to the risk of Cholera, the immigration authorities disallowed the Bandemer's plan to settle in St. Louis. Instead, the family continued as far along the river as they could until finally putting down roots in Minnesota.

Bandemer joined with other German immigrants to found a farm community called Carver. He and his son John (who was officially recognized as the first John Jr.), each received 600 acres of land from a government grant. An intense effort to clear the heavily wooded area ensued, which then allowed them to put their old world carpentry skills into action. One of the barns still stands today even though no nails or screws were used. Instead, all of the boards were firmly fitted together to create balance and leverage.

In addition to his ingenuity, Bandemer was also a man of faith. He was raised German Lutheran and identified himself as a Christian although the denomination wasn't divided like today with a traditional sect and a more modern Evangelical division. Regardless, Bandemer was noted as a man who loved and served people through personal acts of kindness and through the active fellowship of the newly established church in Carver.

Bandemer married his nanny and the two had nine more children. One of those offspring was a son named Charles. When Bandemer died in 1877 at the age of 73, it was Charles who inherited the farm from his father Johann because his older brother John Jr. already had his own 600-acre portion.

Charles Bandemer got married and had a son named Fred. Over time, the father-son relationship became contentious. In 1901, the spelling of the family's last name was changed to Bandimere. It's not known who changed the spelling and why, but it is clearly identifiable in the graveyards in Carver. Around the same time, Fred moved due west to Groton, South Dakota where he attended school to learn business and law and then went to work in a bank. He also met his wife Anna, a talented artist and photographer noted for her ability to colorize photos with watercolors, who owned a photo studio with her sister that was located across the street. The couple married and started a family with daughter Lela arriving in 1906 and son John arriving in 1908. But their stay in South Dakota would be short-lived.

Relief in the Rockies

John Bandimere Sr. was just two years old when his family moved to Colorado in 1910. The change of location was prompted by his mother's severe asthma. When the family lived in South Dakota, she could never lay horizontally. Her husband made a special bed so she could sleep at an angle that would allow her to breathe more comfortably. The dry climate in the Rockies provided a chance for Anna Bandimere to get her life back. Bandimere Sr. inherited his mother's struggles with asthma and suffered through his life because of it, but it wasn't as severe as her condition.

The Bandimere's first stop was in Sugar City, a small statutory town in Crowley County located southeast of Colorado Springs and east of Pueblo. Fred and Anna were among Sugar City's founding families. Fred helped plot the street system, name the streets and structure the town government.

In 1914, they moved to Golden, a suburb just west of Denver. There, Fred Bandimere took on a number of jobs to make ends meet. He was a fruit and vegetable farmer. He was a land developer. And in his work as a part-time lawyer, he provided legal counsel for local citizens and wrote up his own contracts.

His stint as a tax assessor for Jefferson County was one of his most interesting and most difficult jobs.

"He took the worst assignment," David Bandimere recounts.

"He was willing to go into the back hills and the mountainous areas above Golden, clear up into the Continental Divide area, and find people who had improved their properties but had not registered with the county and paid the appropriate taxes. He was a very despised and hated man. He had the gumption and he had the vehicle that allowed him to go up dirt roads and trails."

The commissioners appreciated the additional revenue that Fred Bandimere was bringing into the county and as a show of their gratitude offered to sell him a 320-acre property for just $75. Years later, that land became a piece of what Coloradans now know as Golden Gate Canyon State Park.

Miracle in a Model T

By the time Bandimere Sr. was 14, he was driving vehicles around the farm and subsequently getting more interested in vehicle performance. Having dropped out of school after tenth grade to attend the needs of the family and the farm, the teenager also had a fateful encounter with the owner of the Golden Ford car dealership that led to a special arrangement where he was allowed to take anything he wanted from the dealership's junkyard. Bandimere Sr. eventually had enough parts to embark on the rebuilding of a homemade Model T car.

There was only one problem. The novice mechanic didn't understand welding so he wired the car together instead. Once assembled, he took his handiwork down what today is 44th Avenue in Golden. Predictably, the car came apart and in the chaos he stuck the gearshift right through the fatty part of his right leg. Although Bandimere Sr. was several miles from the farmhouse, a family friend named Ed Churches managed to get him home. His mother Anna, a self-proclaimed doctor, wouldn't allow her son to go to the hospital. Instead, she was able to crudely remove the shifter from his leg and patch up the nasty wound.

That wasn't Bandimere Sr.'s only traumatic experience in a Model T vehicle nor was it the most life threatening. Around 1930, his grandfather Charles Bandimere died a horrific death back in Minnesota. While trying to burn off some dried foliage on his farm, a wind shift pushed the flames back towards him and caught his clothing on fire. He was found burned to death, face down, just a few feet from the main ditch of the farm's watering system.

Charles' family contacted Fred and informed him that they were allowing family members to come back to the farm and claim the items they wanted. Fred sent his sons John (who was in his early 20s) and his younger brother Horace in a Model T pickup to make the 900-mile trek from Golden all the way back to Carver.

The brothers had not yet crossed the state line when they were caught in a ferocious blizzard in Northern Colorado. There was no heater in the truck and the storm was so bad that they were forced to pull over and wait it out.

In those days, the vehicles ran off white gas. Bandimere Sr. and his brother had brought some extra fuel with them along with some matches and a small can. Throughout the night, they kept burning parts and parcels of the white gas until the sun came up the next morning to keep them from freezing.

As the storm cleared, they realized they were a short distance from a farmhouse, but the blizzard was so bad that they couldn't see it. As they approached the home hoping for some warmth and perhaps something to eat, the residents opened the door to the ghastly site of two young men covered in soot from head to toe.

"If they had not carried the extra fuel and if they didn't have the extra matches and a can to put that fuel in, they wouldn't have survived the night," David Bandimere says. "I believe all of those things were God's provision. Otherwise, they would have both been lost in that trip and a lot of things would have stopped right there."

After returning from Minnesota, Bandimere Sr. grew increasingly disinterested in working the fields. His father had become adept at planting and harvesting fruit and vegetable crops including his famously productive cherry and apple orchards. The family also augmented its income with a modest herd of dairy cows. As Horace grew more capable, he started planting corn and sugar beets and took a liking to the very life that his older brother was longing to escape.

It wouldn't be long before Bandimere Sr. would finally get his chance to experience a whole new world where cars roamed free on the big city streets. Endless opportunity surely awaited him in Denver.

3
Love and War

Perhaps Fred Bandimere had been pushed to the limit with his son's mechanical projects that left the farm in disarray. Or maybe John was tired of feeling trapped out in the country when there was seemingly greater opportunity to express his burgeoning curiosity. No one knows for sure. But there's a good chance that both sentiments factored into Bandimere Sr. packing up and moving to downtown Denver.

One other fact, however, likely played a considerable role in the life-changing decision.

In 1930, a 22-year old Bandimere Sr. was still living on the farm but growing increasingly restless. His younger sister Lela was attending Sunday services and school at Denver Bible Institute to be a missionary, so she enjoyed the all Sunday affair that featured traditional ministry along with special teaching from the pastor who was also the head of the school. After the morning service had concluded, attendees would eat a sack lunch and then continue on throughout the rest of the day and into the evening.

There, she befriended a young lady named Frances Penley from Englewood. Much like Bandimere Sr., she too had a fascinating story. In 1886, her father Francis Penley, the son of an English Vicar, immigrated to Boston at the age of 16. He rode the rails to find distant relatives in Sedalia, Colorado. There, he met and married Katherine Eggleston. While living in Sedalia, they had twin girls who were very sick as infants. The only doctor was 13 miles to the north in Littleton. Francis and Katherine never owned or drove a motor vehicle. Their only transportation in the harsh winter of 1910 was Francis' horse drawn buckboard and hindered their access to medical care. Tragically, both babies were lost before the age of three months. When Katherine was pregnant with Frances, she demanded that her husband move them to Englewood, which was much closer to Littleton. She refused to risk the life another child.

The move proved to be a wise one. Frances grew up healthy and as a young woman attended Denver Bible Institute with her father and developed a strong friendship with Lela Bandimere. On many occasions, Lela would come back to the farm and tell her older brother John Sr. about Frances. He eventually decided to go to church one Sunday and see what the fuss was all about.

Things moved rather quickly from there. After meeting around 1931, Bandimere Sr. and Frances eloped in 1933. A judge at the Boulder courthouse married them as Lela and a family friend stood by their sides.

Later that year, the couple took an adventurous trip to the World's Fair in Chicago. While it was certainly filled with marital bliss, Bandimere Sr. undoubtedly became enamored with the impressive display of automotive ingenuity in which American manufacturers introduced wonders such as a V-16 Cadillac limousine, a rear-engine Lincoln, and the futuristic Pierce Silver Arrow. Undoubtedly, the wheels inside his active mind were rapidly turning.

A Sign of Things To Come

When Bandimere Sr. moved to downtown Denver, he immediately began scouring for whatever work he could find.

He met a man who owned a company that mounted large signs for businesses around town. But the man already had three employees and wasn't hiring at the time. That didn't deter Bandimere Sr. who would become known for his persistence.

"You don't have to pay me anything," he told the man. "If I don't prove myself to you, I'll go away. But if you think I'm worthy of having a job, you can hire me."

Over the next several days, Bandimere Sr. put his German heritage work ethic to the test. One of his jobs was to hang a famous sign for an icehouse just off Colfax near the viaduct. That sign stayed securely mounted for over 80 years.

Bandimere Sr. did such efficient and effective work that the business owner fired the three other men and hired him as their one-man replacement. His trademark hardworking spirit would follow him for years to come, but in the meantime, it was his ability to adapt and survive that, like his father Fred, led him into numerous ventures.

One of his first businesses was a car lot that was located on Downing Street. Bandimere Sr. would scavenge the alleys for abandoned, broken down cars, or buy cars from people at a low price. He would then tow them back to his garage where he would fix and restore them before putting them up for sale. Oftentimes, Bandimere Sr. would allow the new owners to pay him while they were already in possession of the car. He also gathered scrap metal and sold it for as much as $100 in one day.

Bandimere Sr. and his wife Frances lived in a small downtown apartment throughout much of the Great Depression into the late 1930s. After selling cars during the day, he would work on people's cars in a garage on the lot late into the evening. It wasn't uncommon for Bandimere Sr. to ask Frances for help to get things done.

"She would take carburetors off the cars or other simple tasks," David Bandimere says. "The first time he asked her to change the oil on a car, he didn't tell her that there was an oil plug and that you drained the oil first. She was lying underneath the car and unbolted the oil pan. It fell down on her and she was soaked in oil."

The couple would get a good laugh out of that story for years to come, but it did serve as a lesson to Bandimere Sr. who realized he needed to be more instructive in the future.

Amid the heavy workload, they also took in Bandimere Sr.'s mother Anna and sister Irene who stayed at their place for a while. Even his brother Horace spent time living with the newlywed couple.

"My mom and dad lived on very little sleep." David Bandimere says. "They had a passion to get things done and they worked incredible amounts of hours. They could live on four or five hours of sleep a night. They had all of these things going on early in their marriage. They didn't have much time to enjoy being a couple."

Life didn't get any simpler. In 1935, Bandimere Sr. and Frances welcomed their first child, daughter Joanna, into the world. But her arrival wasn't without serious complications. Frances suffered a ruptured appendix just prior to delivery and she and her baby weren't expected to live.

"For a long time, we were the miracles of Presbyterian Hospital," Joanna Gager explains. "They told my dad to tell her goodbye."

Frances' appendix had burst so badly that the peritonitis got into Joanna's system. After she was born, she suffered from painful eczema that also covered up her chicken pox symptoms for three months before the doctors realized she had contracted the infectious disease.

"I put my parents through a lot," Gager says. "I was born with all kinds of problems. Dad had to work day and night so they could afford things like treatment and a special milk I had to drink."

The family ultimately survived the distressing episode and three years later, in 1938, welcomed their first son, John Charles Bandimere, Jr. into their hectic life.

"My dad carried my mom up the stairs," Gager recalls. "She was carrying Johnny in a blue blanket. I can see it in my mind. I remember laying by her on the bed as she held this little baby in her arms."

In 1939, two more eventful things took place for the family. Bandimere Sr. opened an auto shop on Broadway Street with partner Marty Keller. The family also moved to a house on Benton Street in the Denver suburb of Wheat Ridge. Throughout the next few years, it was a constant flow of activity around the Bandimere household and the shop.

"Everything was work for my dad–his job, his fun, his hobbies," Gager says. "He just liked to work–day and night."

Active Duty

While most Americans were still recovering from the effects of economic collapse tied to the Stock Market crash of 1929, trouble was brewing across Atlantic Ocean in Western Europe. In September of 1939, Adolph Hitler's German Army invaded Poland and set into motion a series of events that would ultimately lead to World War II.

After remaining neutral for the better part of two years, the United States formally sided with the Allied nations that included Great Britain, France, Russia and Poland. In April of 1941, U.S. forces saw their first combat action against the increasingly aggressive Axis Powers. Germany, Italy and Japan had differing interests yet somehow found common ground within their individual hopes for totalitarian rule.

By the time the Japanese attacked Pearl Harbor on December 7, 1941, the United States military was fully engaged in the global battle that would shape the geo-political landscape for decades. Of the 16.1 million Americans called into active duty, 291,557 didn't make it home alive while another 671,846 returned as wounded warriors.

John Bandimere Sr. was not one of those men. His younger brother Horace also did not serve, but his youngest brother David did.

Bandimere Sr. was held back due to a heart condition that had ailed him since birth, but he likely would have been shielded from the draft regardless. The war department was keeping men with mechanical talents home to assist with some of their machinery. For Bandimere Sr., that meant spending a required amount of time each week helping the families whose husbands and fathers were gone with their automotive needs.

Although gas was being rationed severely, his status with the government allowed him to have all the fuel he needed. During the day, he would teach women how to change their tires or change the oil. Sometimes, Bandimere Sr. would give instruction at the Emily Griffith Opportunity School in downtown Denver where his wife would serve as his assistant.

At night, Bandimere Sr. would make his living working on cars. As had become necessary, Frances often did her part to help bear some of the burdensome workload. And while serving a unique form of active duty was personally rewarding, it also opened doors that would lead into the next phase of his life.

4

Supercharged

During World War II and shortly thereafter its ending in 1945, John Bandimere Sr. enjoyed a unique relationship with the United States military. He had access to government auctions where he was able to purchase high-grade materials at a low cost. He was also allowed to pick through war surplus and take items home for free. No one had finer aluminum than the military, so Bandimere Sr. would melt down airplane propellers and turrets and use the raw material in his foundry at the shop on Benton Street.

Government officials sometimes simply gave him things they no longer needed such as a large collection of unused combat boots, which he advertised and sold to the public. Whereas others saw junk, Bandimere Sr. saw potential. And he carried that unique vision into his burgeoning career as a car performance guru.

Performance Pioneer

Bandimere Sr.'s military connections helped feed an obsession with high altitude performance that had been gaining steam for several years. By 1936, his tinkering led to the creation of a snowmobile that proceeded Hetteen, Hoist & Derrick Co.'s first attempt by 19 years. Later known as Polaris Industries, the company did not successfully produce a commercial model until 1955. Any earlier designs were crude representations that had emerged from Canada and northern States like Wisconsin and South Dakota during the early 1900s.

And then there's the curious case of the superchargers. Making claims about being the first to invent something or the first to accomplish a notable feat can be precarious business. This is certainly the case with Bandimere Sr. and his historical work with blowers.

Ever since German inventor Karl Benz introduced the modern automobile in 1886, mechanics and engineers have been trying to find ways to make them go faster. Bandimere Sr. had caught the speed bug on his father's farm and continued that fascination throughout most of his life. But prior to the 1930s, the concept of using an air compressor to increase the air pressure supplied to an internal combustion engine was mostly being explored in Europe – that is except for the work Bandimere Sr. was doing in his shop.

"Dad was supercharging flatheads in the '30s," David Bandimere says. "He would have been one of the first people in the United States to design a way to put a war blower onto a conventional gas engine with a V-belt design. With his foundry, he had the ability to create the pulleys and other parts that he needed. Some of those pulleys would take up to six V-belts in order to try to hold it all together."

In 1937, the McCulloch Engineering Company based in Milwaukee, Wisconsin, began selling a flathead supercharger unit. Bandimere Sr. would soon thereafter become a distributor for the product and would install them onto the cars of his clients, which were often wealthy businessmen. Superchargers were notorious for burning up the engine, but Bandimere Sr. figured out a way to keep them alive before the factories could come up with a solution.

After the family moved to Benton Street in Wheat Ridge, his inventive spirit soared. The family believes that he was likely one of the first engineers to put a Cadillac V8 engine in an earlier model Ford. He called it a "Fordillac."

Bandimere Sr. also came up with an idea to mount two V8 engines back-to-back but couldn't quite figure out how to run them off the same crank. One morning, he woke up and was excited as a little kid on Christmas morning.

"I've got it! I know how to do it!" he proclaimed.

"Dad would go to bed with a problem on his mind and he would wake up with the answers," David Bandimere says. "He had this God-given ability to solve problems in his sleep."

But in the wake of whatever project he was working on at the time, things were usually a substantial mess. Bandimere Sr. didn't have time to clean up. He was too busy solving the world's problems, so to speak.

"To go in the shop was just awful at times," David Bandimere recalls. "He would work off of his lathe to the point where shavings were everywhere. I don't even know how he could get in there to work. If you cleaned for him, it wasn't that he didn't appreciate it, but then he couldn't find things. Somehow he knew how to find things in the biggest messes."

But Bandimere Sr.'s inability to efficiently organize his garage paled in comparison to the physical pain he suffered due to his lack of knowledge regarding the ill effects of sustained exposure to carbon monoxide.

"In the winters, when they had to work around the clock, he would run a car to tune it, but he didn't exhaust it," David Bandimere says. "Today you go to most dealerships or garages and they have hoses they hook up to the exhausts and they run the fumes outside the building. But dad didn't do that and he got carbon monoxide poisoning and suffered for most of his adult years with horrendous headaches. I saw my dad at times just scream in pain. He would get down on the floor and literally bang his head on the floor just trying to get some kind of relief. With all the gifted things he was able to do, he suffered most of the time."

The Architect

It was rare to find Bandimere Sr. doing something other than work, but in what little spare time he afforded himself, he could usually be found spending it with young people. Among those activities was a Sunday School class that he taught throughout the early 1940s at Sheridan Evangelical Church on 32nd and Zenobia.

Bill Vincent, one of the regular teenage attendees, invited his 16-year old friend David Beckman to join the group. Soon thereafter, the two started showing up at the Bandimere shop on Benton where they grew increasingly fascinated with all things automotive.

"When I was in John's shop, I had my head in the engine," Beckman reminisced six weeks before his death on March 6, 2014. "I was down in it as deep as I could get. He would let us take engines apart, but he wouldn't let us put them back together."

Beckman also recalled taking care of Bandimere Sr.'s children who were always "running around" the house and the garage, and reflected on fond memories of Frances Bandimere.

"Frances was a sweet lady," he said. "She was a very committed Christian. She had a big influence on me. She let me work in the kitchen. I can remember to this day what it was like to be in that tiny kitchen. She was always fun."

Of course, fun with Bandimere Sr. usually involved cars although for Beckman and Vincent it didn't always seem that way.

"I remember when we went out on West 32nd Avenue way out past Wadsworth Boulevard and down the hill," Beckman explained. "It was a dirt road back then. John drove so fast. Bill Vincent and I were in the backseat and scared to death. What could we do? We hung on for all it was worth."

In another instance, Bandimere Sr. drove the teenagers southeast towards the old airfield. Along the way, he caught up with another car. As the quarter mile long road came to a close, Bandimere Sr. was practically pushing the other driver out of the way, and it made his passengers more than nervous.

"Bill and I were really scared then," Beckman said. "John Sr. would take chances like that. That's how he was. He was a speed maniac. He was fearless."

And the adventures didn't always take place in cars. On one occasion, Bandimere Sr. and the boys went to Inspiration Point to ride bicycles down the hill. Bandimere Sr. wanted to try out a new gear that he put on Beckman's bike. Unfortunately, they couldn't see the ditch that awaited them below. Traveling at a healthy speed, Bandimere Sr. ran right into the ditch and "went head over heels."

The wreck did significant damage to the back of Bandimere Sr.'s neck, which, along with the carbon monoxide poisoning he already had, added to his severe headaches. It even impacted his ability to work under cars. He could no longer hold his head up on a creeper.

That was just how Bandimere Sr. lived his life—with reckless abandon. And Beckman loved that about the man. But he grew to love something even more than his spontaneous spirit or his creative genius or his mechanical mind. Over time, he began to have a stronger appreciation for Bandimere Sr.'s passion for the Bible and his desire to see others enter into a relationship with Jesus Christ.

That subtle influence helped Beckman make a life-changing

decision during his senior year in high school. That year, he lost his young cousin and his brother within a month of each other. His brother, in fact, died a week before Christmas. One Sunday, he was helping his Aunt Hette wash dishes when she told Beckman he should go downstairs to his room and listen to a radio program called The Lutheran Hour that featured prominent minister Dr. Walter A. Maier.

Beckman was happy to get out of doing the dishes, so he promptly did as his Aunt suggested. At the end the message, Meyer gave his audience very clear instructions:

"If you're driving, pull over and dedicate your life to the Lord," he said. *"If you're in your room at home, dedicate your life to the Lord."*

Beckman got off his bed and ran over to the door and locked it. He then ran over to the window and pulled the shades down. Beckman returned to his bed and knelt on the floor and prayed:

"Lord, you can have my life."

With those simple words, everything changed. Although he struggled in high school, he exceeded his own expectations by earning a degree from Wheaton College, then Columbia University graduate school, then Dallas Seminary undergraduate and graduate school.

When Beckman returned to Denver, he entered into a career in college administration and was directly responsible for a series of mergers that resulted in the creation of Colorado Christian College, which has since become known as Colorado Christian University. When he first took over as president there, the school had just 28 students and four graduating seniors. By the spring of 2013, CCU housed 4,000 students and graduated 431.

Beckman's only A during his senior year at Wheat Ridge High School was mechanical drawing. He loved to draw buildings and originally had hoped to pursue a career in architecture. But later in life, a man would astutely remark that God had made Beckman "an architect of students."

Ironically, it was a Sunday School teacher and mechanical architect of sorts whose real classroom was in the garage that ultimately had one of the most profound impacts on a future so-called architect's life.

"John's influence helped to prepare my heart to accept Christ,"

Beckman said. "If Bill Vincent had not invited me to that Sunday School class, I doubt that I would have done what I've done for the Lord. John Sr. affected my life in an extraordinary way."

5
Speed Racer

Of the many young guys that hung around the parts store at 803 Champa Street, several found themselves initiated into a smaller circle of performance enthusiasts that would gather regularly at Bandimere Sr.'s shop on Benton Street.

Allan Perotin was among that group. He was 19 years old when he started working at the shop and getting more than just instruction about cars.

"A lot of times before we'd start working, we would have a prayer meeting in the morning," Perotin recalls. "John would read out of the Bible and then he would pray."

After that, however, it was all about the engines. And Perotin learned everything he ever wanted to know about the inner workings of an automobile and more.

"John was a great teacher," he says. "I learned a lot of my mechanical knowledge through him. There wasn't anything that man couldn't do. I was always amazed at the things he could accomplish working on the milling machine or in the foundry. He had a great mechanical mind."

Before long, Perotin and the tight-knit group were caught up in Bandimere Sr.'s racing pursuits. And it turned out to be one crazy ride.

The Race To The Clouds

In 1916, an entrepreneur and venture capitalist from Colorado Spring named Spencer Penrose had just finished widening the road allowing drivers to travel to the top of Pikes Peak. To help promote tourism, he created a race that has since become known as The Pikes Peak International Hill Climb, or as he famously dubbed it, "The Race To The Clouds."

As Bandimere Sr. was getting caught up in the speed and performance world, the progressively more popular event provided an exciting opportunity to see how his supercharged engines stacked up against the seasoned car owners of the day.

By then, he and Frances had moved to Wheat Ridge. Joanna and John Jr. were already around, but David had yet to be born. Bandimere Sr.'s first attempt at the Pikes Peak Hill Climb was around 1939 or 1940. But he didn't decide to compete in the race until less than two weeks before it was set to start. That first car was nicknamed "The Old Foo," because of the foolishness that surrounded its creation.

"They built the car in 10 or 12 days," Bandimere Jr. explains. "He never went to bed. He stayed out in the garage nonstop and worked on it."

Once it was time for the race, Bandimere Sr. loaded the car on a trailer and pulled it to Pikes Peak. Frances drove so her husband could sleep on the way down in the back seat. Amazingly, he had the energy and wherewithal to complete the 12.42-mile race that included 156 turns.

But that was the only time he would serve as his own driver. He brought Hugh Thomas with him for the next few attempts and later partnered with Gordon Herring. Regardless of who was driving, the Pikes Peak Hill Climb quickly became his favorite race.

"Everything shut down at the Benton Street shop while cars were prepared for the race," Bandimere Jr. says. "At the climb, dad handled the mechanical chores and was always tinkering with a new combination."

Allan Perotin was there to experience the controlled chaos firsthand.

"We didn't get much sleep the week before the race when we drove down there to practice," he says. "We'd have a problem with the car and at night he would lay down and you'd swear he was asleep. But a little bit later, he would get up and say, 'I've got the answer!' Evidently he was just laying there thinking about it until he came up with a solution."

In those first races, the mechanic rode with the driver in an open wheel car that was oddly fitted with two seats. This was also true in Indy racing. This way, if there was a mechanical problem along the way, the car could potentially be fixed so it could finish the race. It also allowed for some unique testing opportunities.

"I had some hairy rides up Pikes Peak in that car with John," Perotin says. "We'd be rolling around and the car would start to slide out. You'd see a thousand-foot drop when you started coming to the end. It was kind of scary."

Much like his first attempt at the mountain, Bandimere Sr. usually wouldn't get the urge to race the event until late in the process and sometimes because the money just wasn't available. He and his crew would travel down to Colorado Springs a week before the race for early morning practices.

A few years later, Bandimere Sr. partnered with driver Gordon Herring for some races around 1956 and 1957. He had purchased a Cummins Diesel Indy car that had raced at the Indianapolis 500 in 1952 and 1953. Bandimere Sr., John Jr., and David, took the GMC Cadillac Truck to Los Angeles and towed back this very special car. Bandimere Sr.'s dream was to convert it from a two-wheel drive to a four-wheel drive for the Pikes Peak Hill Climb. Prior to this event, he had already been the first engineer to build a 4x4 car for that race.

It was too late to finish the Cummins Diesel car for the 1956 "Race To The Clouds," so the old two-seater was prepared to run one last time. When the Bandimere crew arrived, the race officials refused to allow the car that Bandimere Sr. had run up the hill so many times because it was "out of style," so they said. The crew sped back to Denver and worked all night to try to finish the Cummins car instead.

"They put it together so fast, it was able to run but I don't even know if it finished the race that year," David Bandimere says. "There were too many problems to work out."

No matter what the situation, Perotin was always impressed with Bandimere Sr.'s ability to consistently stand toe-to-toe with the competition.

"What amazed me was the fact that we were always able to compete at the top against outfits that had a lot of money to spend," Perotin remarks. "We were always bare bones."

South of the Border

On occasion, Bandimere Sr. would venture outside of the greater Denver area to feed his craving for competitive racing. But it wasn't just trips to the south in Colorado Springs for the Pikes Peak climb. In the early 1950s, he heard about an exciting road race that had inaugurated in 1950 following the completion of the Mexican section of the Pan-American Highway. The Carrera Panamericana, or the Mexican road race, as U.S. competitors commonly called it, was a border-to-border event that ran until dangerous conditions led to its demise in 1954. The race was revived in 1988 and a safer version of its predecessor continues to run annually today.

Originally staged as a race that ran from the north to the south, the course was changed in 1951 to start near Tuxtla and finish in Juarez. The total distance was an estimated 2,096 miles and was usually completed in about 18 hours but spread out over eight stages. Some of the notable racing names that participated included NASCAR founder Bill France Sr., and stock car drivers Curtis Turner and Hershel McGriff. There was also a strong Central American and European contingency.

Bandimere Sr. took his one and only shot at Mexican glory with driver Jack Latham and a young Allan Perotin as his assistant. The three adventurers traveled from the Southern U.S. border down to the Guatemalan border for the start of the race. They raced through Oaxaca and Tuxtla and Puebla and on to Mexico City. At the end of each stage, the crew would have a couple of hours to work on the car before race officials impounded the vehicle.

"We were competing against the race teams from different manufacturers," Perotin recalls. "Lincoln had a driver from Indianapolis and a semi-truck that housed a complete shop. They had rear ends and air compressors and all kinds of parts hanging on the wall. And we did everything by hand."

Perotin also remembers the incredible surroundings. At the time, Mexico was very undeveloped. They would drive through villages and see people washing their clothes in the lake. At night, one of the men would have to keep watch.

"Cattle would be sleeping on the road because it was warmer,"

Perotin says. "I also remember John bargaining with a Mexican woman for a blanket one day. It was an experience of a lifetime."

Latham was driving well early on and had Bandimere Sr.'s car in second place. But he lost control on a turn, crashed into a straw barrier and tore up the front end. The front was torn up, Bandimere Sr. and Perotin had to wait until the next day before they could drive to Latham's location. They were driving separately in a Ford sedan and were not allowed on the road during the race stages.

"You couldn't even run across the road," Perotin says. "There were soldiers sitting along the roadside and they would shoot at you."

Mechanics were supposedly allowed to do anything to the car to make it safer for the race. Prior to entering Mexico, Bandimere Sr. and Perotin had removed the Cadillac's bench seat and replaced it with a bucket seat. When they got to Mexico City, officials told them that the modification wasn't allowed.

"We had to borrow a front seat from a Cadillac dealer in Mexico City," Perotin says. "When we came back after the car cracked up, we took the seat out and shipped it back. From Juarez to Denver, I drove the car sitting on my toolbox."

The Denver Drags

If a driver around Denver was known to own a car that ran well in the 1930s and 1940s, there was a good chance he would be tested at random street corners. Everyone wanted to check him out and see how fast his car could go. This was especially true of someone like Bandimere Sr.

Over the years, David Bandimere has encountered several fellows who were young men during that era. They have told him stories about meeting his mom and dad throughout the city and challenging them to a spontaneous drag race. Most of the stories ended the same. After getting soundly beat by the Bandimere car, they would follow them home to find out what was under their hood.

Until 1951, nothing had been formalized amongst the local speed enthusiasts. That's when Jim McKindley organized what is believed to be the first official drag race. It took place on Ridge Road and included the cooperation of the Sheriff's Department who blocked off the county road and diverted traffic.

It was actually a common practice for the authorities to do their part to keep things safe. Fred Bandimere was known in the county for his work as a tax assessor and for his legal work in the court-house. So when Bandimere Sr., Bandimere Jr., and other hot rodders were roaming the streets, the police would block off certain streets and allow grudge matches or an occasional test race.

"In the early days of drag racing, they used a flag starter," David Bandimere says. "They'd put a guy out in the middle between the two cars. He had a series of colored flags that he would point at the cars and then he would throw up the green flag to start the race. Then they had to have people at the finish line that would be the witnesses of who actually went across the line first."

Bandimere knows first hand because as a kid he would some-times go with his dad to these races and "experience the incredible rush when he took off." But as good as Bandimere Sr.'s cars were, he didn't always win.

One evening in 1957, a young man named Jim Taylor stopped at West 32nd Avenue in his '56 Corvette. Alongside him pulled up Bandimere Sr. who was driving a '57 Chevy sedan. Bandimere Sr. revved his car's engine a few times trying to get Taylor's attention.

"Well, this fellow is acting like he wants to race," Taylor thought to himself. *"I think he's bitten off more than he can chew, but if he wants to go, we'll go."*

At the next stop sign, they both took off. Taylor's slightly mod-ified car was lighter and had a little more horsepower than Bandimere Sr.'s. The race wasn't much of a contest.

"After racing, we stopped and he congratulated me on how well my car ran," Taylor says. "I must have given him my phone number because later on, he invited me to help him at the old Burt Chevrolet dealership in Englewood. He had hooked up with General Motors and was working on a '57 Corvette that was going to go to Nassau for a sports car race there."

When Bandimere Sr. went to the Bahamas, he was mechanical-ly in charge of one Corvette while the famed Zora Arkus Duntov was in charge of the rest of the Corvette field. Bandimere Sr.'s Corvette was the only one that finished the race.

Bandimere Sr. and Taylor's relationship grew from there. Taylor helped install superchargers and did tune ups at the shop on Benton

Street for a few months. He also assisted Bandimere Sr. with a few Pikes Peak race cars before moving to Missouri in 1965.

"John was very intelligent and very interesting," Taylor says. "He knew performance and how to make a car perform. I learned an awful lot from him."

Great Bend and the Black Box

From the late 1930s throughout the 1950s, Bandimere Sr. had become Denver's resident expert on superchargers. This gave him a decided edge against whatever competition he might face on the streets or the area speedways. But the early McCulloch superchargers had a problem. Serious competitors had to constantly replace the ball bearings that became burned and would seize up at high RPMs.

Bob McCulloch was trying to come up with a more reliable design that would also put out more boost. The result of his effort was a blower he called "the black box." It worked very efficiently but it was too expensive to make and too big and impractical for street racing. McCulloch had no use for his prototype so he gave it to Bandimere Sr. who was more than happy to put it to work.

The black box made its first appearance in Great Bend, Kansas, at the National Hot Rod Association's first national event—the 1955 U.S. Nationals. There, he teamed up with Gordon Herring who drove Bandimere Sr.'s '55 Chevy. Today, the famous black box is operating in Bandimere Jr.'s son Sporty Bandimere's 1955 Chevy.

Herring was a truck driver and owned a fleet of semi-trucks. This gave Bandimere Sr. an idea. He converted a 40-foot trailer into a transport unit for his car as well as living quarters and a place to prepare food. In essence, he had created motorsports' first hauler. When Bandimere Sr. arrived with his wife Frances and Herring, it created quite a stir amongst the competitors and the press. In fact, Hot Rod and Car Craft magazines both featured pictures of the trailer in their January editions.

Bandimere Sr. and Herring used 55-gallon drums of racing fuel to support wood planks that allowed the car to drive in and out of the trailer.

"I always joke that I was the first in the sport to use an 18-wheeler like an RV coach," legendary Funny Car driver John Force says. "I built it because I was a truck driver and I could sleep in the trailer. But then I looked at some pictures from John Bandimere Jr.'s portfolio and I saw that his dad had a car that came out of the back of this old 18-wheeler long before anyone else was doing it."

Like The Hatfields and the McCoys

Bandimere Sr. didn't go to all of the races, but rest assured, if someone from Kenz & Leslie was there, so was he.

Bill Kenz and Roy Leslie first opened shop in 1938 and it didn't take long for a highly competitive rivalry to materialize between Bandimere Sr. and the upstart automotive parts and services company. Both were trying to carve out their space in the growing speed and car performance community throughout Denver. That led to numerous encounters on the streets and at the speedways where midget cars and sprint cars were regularly raced.

Tensions were relatively low in the beginning. Bandimere Sr. was focused on Pikes Peak and straightaway racing while Kenz & Leslie had jumped into oval racing. But by the early 1950s, the desire to prove who had the best stuff came to a head.

The 1951 Thanksgiving Day race on Ridge Road, in fact, was partly organized in order to give Bandimere Sr. a chance to test out his blown roadster against his rivals. Ron Leslie was just a kid back then, but he clearly remembers that race as his father and his business partner Kenz went all out trying to keep up.

"That stretch of Ridge Road is right behind where our building is now," Leslie recalls. "It was the crack of dawn and everybody was out there running real hard. John was running the best of the bunch. His car was very light. I remember we took everything we could off that car to make it lighter–the doors, the trunk lid, the hood, the radiator, the shell. And he still beat us. We really got after it."

The race was so exciting that Bandimere Sr.'s daughter Joanna ran the entire distance of the road to tell her dad the good news.

But sometimes the tenacious effort on both sides was too much to handle like the time the fierce competitors faced off at the Centennial horse race track in Littleton.

"John Sr. brought out his Pikes Peak race car with a Cadillac engine in it," Leslie says. "We had built a two-engine car to run out there. John launched his car and did a neutral drop. Belts went everywhere and he ran 69 miles an hour. When it was our turn, we made a decent pass but couldn't get it out of gear when we got to the other end. We had literally welded the flywheel, pressure plate and disc into one chunk. It became a very competitive thing with the Bandimeres and the Kenz & Leslie group, very competitive."

As Ron Leslie got more involved in his father's company and John Jr. and David Bandimere did the same with their auto parts store, the contentiousness continued to swell.

"It was like a hostile relationship," Leslie says. "It was like the Hatfields and the McCoys."

Much later, as the Bandimere family moved away from the parts business, both sides realized how childish they had been all of those years.

"Geez, what a bunch of jerks we were fighting each other so hard," Leslie admits. "It was not intentional. We were all influenced by our parents to a certain degree. Over the years, things have mellowed considerably. John and I get along quite well and I have nothing but respect for everything they have accomplished as a family."

Midget Mastery

As much as Bandimere Sr. loved racing the mountain, on the open road, or along impromptu drag strips in Denver, they were no comparison to his affinity for midget cars and sprint cars.

There wasn't much racing going on during World War II but things picked up quickly thereafter in the late 1940s. Most of the races took place at Lakeside Speedway but other action could be found at Merchant's Park and even outside the state in places like Cheyenne, Wyoming.

Bandimere Sr.'s fire was fueled by his partnership with Ray Koch, the first Harley Davidson dealer in Colorado, who was appropriately known throughout Denver as "The Motorcycle King." Koch owned and drove a red midget car that dominated much of the competition.

"Dad and Ray had this great chemistry," David Bandimere says.

"Dad was a phenomenal wrench and Ray was a fearless driver. They just won. They were a winning machine."

Bandimere Sr. also ran sprint cars at Englewood Speedway and Lakeside with driver Bob Olds and later ran midget cars with drivers Buddy Martinson and Roy Bowe.

But his hobby quickly became an addiction. He had seemingly mastered the world of midget cars, but in truth, midget cars had mastered him. It would take a near tragic event in his family to break him of the habit.

6
Sunday Drive

John Bandimere Sr. was a self-admitted workaholic. Time meant nothing to him. This was especially true during and just after World War II. During the war, he spent every waking hour either working at his shop on Broadway or teaching women how to maintain their vehicles. After the war, his time was consumed with a parts store on Champa Street, special projects in his shop on Benton, or racing cars on the streets, and midget and sprint cars wherever a flag was being dropped.

If his young children wanted to see him, they usually had to go to the garage in the evenings and hope that he had time to say hello. Equally troubling was his neglect of church related activities especially due to the competitive midget and sprint car events that took place on Sundays.

Racing had become his god. But not for long.

A Child's Cry

In 1945, John and Frances added one final member to their family. When David Francis Bandimere was born, polio was rampant across the United States. The crippling virus attacked hundreds of thousands of children, mostly under the age of five, until Jonas Salk famously discovered a vaccine in 1952.

But in 1947, 18 months after his birth, David contracted spinal meningitis, an even more dangerous disease that at that time often resulted in death. For three days, he was in critical condition. For several days after, his parents weren't allowed to go into his room. They had to look through a window to see him.

Perhaps even worse was the crude treatment method that the young child had to endure. He was strapped down to a gurney and then had medicine injected into his spine with a hypodermic needle through his tailbone. There was no way to deaden the pain.

"They could hear me screaming all over the hospital," David Bandimere says.

John Bandimere Jr. was only nine years old at the time, but he vividly remembers the day his younger brother was taken from the house and transported to the hospital.

"He was a blueish color," he recalls. "That was the night that mom and dad came back and prayed. To this day, I can't tell you why they chose to pray in the bathroom, but they knelt by the tub and prayed. That's when my dad told God that he would never race on Sundays again if He spared his son."

Bandimere Sr. could hardly withstand the traumatic events of that day. The thought of losing his son was severe enough. But then hearing his child's cry as he suffered such agonizing pain pushed him to his knees. He was ready to get his priorities in order.

"Lord, take away the smell of exhaust from my nostrils on Sundays," he humbly requested.

David miraculously survived, but the next several months were difficult. The toddler was set back in his development and required special attention as he learned to crawl and talk. Over the years, he has heard people refer to his father's decision not to race on Sundays as a religious decision. But it went much deeper than that.

"It wasn't about a holy, magical, mystical day," he explains. "Dad was addicted to racing and a lot of that took place on Sunday. He didn't dare even smell the fuel or go near the track. He wanted to set a better example as the spiritual leader in his family. He felt like my illness was God's wakeup call for him to rethink his priorities. He wasn't going to allow his passion for racing to get in the way of him worshipping the Lord and spending time with his family."

Passion and Purpose

When David Bandimere was a young man, his father opened up to him about the fateful events that took place in 1947.

"All I lived for was to race," he admitted.

But after his son's life was spared, Bandimere Sr. discovered a renewed passion for people and performance, and an even greater sense of purpose. This was especially true with his wife Frances. If she walked into the shop, everything stopped.

"He had so much love for her and so much respect for her and her presence," David Bandimere says. "The moment she was in his space, she got his full attention."

And then there was the growing contingency of young men—some teenagers, others in their 20s—that regularly stopped by the garage on Benton or the parts store at 803 Champa that Bandimere Sr. had opened in 1946—a converted house that for a while still had three families living upstairs.

"I really want young people to know how to fix their cars right," he often recited.

Bandimere Sr. had grown frustrated with the manufacturers that claimed their products could do such amazing things. He would try them out himself and find out that it wasn't true.

"He rejected the typical mechanical mentality of just throwing parts at things and just wasting people's money," David Bandimere says. "And that just worked perfectly with his passion for young people. Mom and dad always had coffee and donuts in a little lounge upstairs and guys would hang around there on their lunch hour or after work."

One of the earlier arrivals was a young man named Bob Janowski who first met Bandimere Sr. at Lakeside Speedway in 1947. He had just built a home on 46th and Osceola in North Denver and could hear the engines a few blocks away on Sheridan Boulevard as he sat atop his roof while covering his shingles with linseed oil and graphite.

It was in a more personal setting back at the Bandimere residence on Benton Street, however, where Janowski learned a lot about cars. He would drop by, sometimes late at night, to see what Bandimere Sr. was working on.

"I had an open offer to use all of his machinery," Janowski says. "If I didn't still have on my work clothes, there was always a pair of coveralls at the shop for me to use."

Janowski marveled at Bandimere Sr.'s equipment. He had an upright mill that was perfect for milling flat surfaces. He also had a lathe with a six-foot bed and a back-geared and thread-cutting head. It had three sizes of chucks and several styles of tailstocks.

One day, Janowski arrived at the shop at the same time as a driver who was bringing his 18-wheel 400 HP diesel truck to Bandimere Sr.'s for some repairs. The truck had a five-inch exhaust pipe that extended well beyond the cab roof. It was impossible to drive the truck into the shop, so Janowski suggested they cut the pipe off.

"The truck driver was pretty upset," he says. "After John did the work on the engine, I welded the exhaust pipe back together. I think it actually looked better afterward."

But as much as Janowski learned from Bandimere Sr. about automotive engineering, it was the spiritual lessons that were the most valuable.

"John was a loving, kind, man of God," he reflects. "He wouldn't tolerate swearing and he would not gossip. He was a Baptist and I'm a Lutheran, so we had many interesting discussions about Baptism. I had been raised attending Bible studies, but John taught me how to study my Bible. His devotion to Christ as his Savior and leader was the biggest reason that his shop was such a nice place to be."

It was a few years later in the late 1950s, when a young Naval veteran named John Abbott started hanging out at the drive-ins where he met John Bandimere Jr. That naturally led him to Bandimere Sr. where he found an ally in his quest for speed. Abbott, who was 21 years old at the time, started buying parts from the store on Champa and getting help from Bandimere Sr. at the shop on Benton.

"I was always wanting to experiment with something new and that was where you went, to John Sr.," Abbott says. "I was probably one of the first guys to have a 348 engine in my '59 Chevy. I wanted to hop it up. Nobody knew how to bore those engines because the angle of the block was different from a typical V-8 engine. John Sr. had to make special plates to bore it and was a big help in my early racing days."

Abbott went on to have a highly successful career from the late 1950s into the 1980s including Top Fuel Dragster titles in 1977 at the Hot Rod Magazine Championships and in 1978 at the International Hot Rod Association's Spring Nationals. His biggest single accomplishment took place in 1981 when he won the NHRA U.S. Nationals. In 2006, Abbott was inducted into the Colorado

Motorsports Hall of Fame. In 2014, he received the same honor from the International Drag Racing Hall of Fame, which was founded by racing legend "Big Daddy" Don Garlits.

Of the young men that came into the Bandimere's life, Mark Williams had one of the most unique experiences. While in his early teens, he lived two blocks away and would make frequent bike rides to mess around with an old sprint car that Bandimere Sr. had sitting around his shop. Williams moved away at the age of 15, but by 1963, he was married and living across the street in a small apartment with his wife and two children. He came back to Wheat Ridge after reconnecting with Bandimere Sr. at the store on Champa Street and taking a job in his Benton Street shop.

Williams was working there on November 22, 1963, the day President John F. Kennedy was assassinated. It was a tumultuous time in American history yet an exciting time to be around the car scene in Denver. Much of that revolved around Bandimere Sr.'s bent towards innovation.

"John Sr. had a ton of ideas," Williams recalls. "He had way more unique ideas than he could ever get done. There was a new project every day. Very few things ever actually got through to completion. But that was just his genius. He was so full of ideas."

Williams also benefitted from a tubing bender that Bandimere Sr. had acquired during World War II. He had bought his own race car and during his spare time would use the device to work on it at the shop. He later sold that car and used the money to start Mark Williams Enterprises, which now is a prominent manufacturer that builds many of the rear ends, axles and drive shafts for racers across the country.

While Bandimere Sr. made a significant impact on the professional futures of several young men during that time, his biggest contributions were often spiritual in nature. The door to such conversation was usually opened during those times when difficult personal circumstances arose.

"If you walked into his space and you had a problem or a heartache in your life, he dropped everything," David Bandimere says.

In those moments, his wife Frances was an effective partner as she showed them love through a motherly hug or by holding their hands. She would look into the eyes of these young men, many which were rough around the edges, and express the love of Christ to them.

"Honey, I love you," she would say. "Do you know my Jesus?"

Often, her sweet appeal worked in concert with the unique ways that Bandimere Sr. shared spiritual truths using mechanical and car-related analogies. For instance, he would use the concept of the supercharger to convey a message about the Holy Spirit:

"You might be alive just like a car has an engine and is running," *Bandimere Sr. often taught. "But there's no real power. You bring the Lord into your life and it's like hooking a supercharger up to your engine. Now you have real power. You have power that most people don't get to experience. When the Lord is in your life, you have the power to deal with life and heartache. You have the power to live with patience and to love people and you learn how to respond to those that abuse you."*

Bandimere Sr. also told a story about a friend who bought a race car that had no engine. The man would enjoy sitting in the car, but without an engine he couldn't go anywhere. After setting the stage, Bandimere Sr. would then ask young people this profound question:

"Without the Lord, how can you go anywhere in life?"

Beyond Benton

Bandimere Sr.'s passion for influencing young hearts didn't stop in those infrequent moments when he stepped away from the shop on Benton or his store on Champa. In the late 1940s, he discovered some new ways to share God's love with others through Gideons International.

In 1899, Samuel E. Hill, John H. Nicohlson and William J. Knights founded the evangelical organization at a YMCA in Janesville, Wisconsin, where they discussed the need for Bible distribution throughout the United States. Many of the original volunteers were young professionals or retired businessmen.

Having just experienced a spiritual epiphany, the timing was perfect for Bandimere Sr. to align himself with a missions-minded group that would become known for placing Bibles in hotels, hospi-

tals, medical offices, schools, colleges, prisons and even on the bat-
tlefield.

"Dad was a great believer in the power of the Word of God,"
David Bandimere says. "He loved the stories of the difference the
Bible made by being in the motel rooms and the stories that came
back from the frontlines of war."

Bandimere Sr. remained active with the Gideons for the rest of
his life. He was a formative spokesperson and would share the vision
with churches and youth groups throughout Denver.

It was a lesser-known interest, however, that led him to one of
his most fascinating ministry opportunities. It wasn't common
knowledge, but earlier in life Bandimere Sr. had fostered a strong
desire to become a doctor. He was fascinated with the human body
and would often make comparisons between anatomical and automotive concepts. The heart, for instance, was like the oil pumping in
an engine.

Bandimere Sr. was never squeamish around blood and guts.
That distinct trait, coupled with his great affinity for the men and
women who fought in World War II and the Korean War and his
status as a Gideon, opened the door to meaningful interaction with
wounded veterans at Fitzsimons Army Medical Center in Aurora.

Bandimere Sr. in essence became a volunteer chaplain. On
Sunday afternoons and evenings, he would walk the halls and spend
time encouraging and praying for the fallen soldiers there. After a
while, the staff became increasingly comfortable with his presence
and would allow him to come into the surgery room."

"He would love on those young people and share the Lord with
them and hold their hands and just be there for them," David
Bandimere says. "He was allowed tremendous freedom. Only the
Lord knows how many he brought to Christ during those years."

His three children loved hearing the reports of his experiences
and how God had used him in the lives of those hurting servicemen.

Bandimere Sr. continued his ministry at the hospital until the
wave of wounded slowed down in the late 1950s. But that didn't
keep him from finding other outlets for ministry. In fact, Bandimere
Sr. was also an excellent singer with a capable tenor voice. He sang
at funerals and at church with David whom he taught, along with

John Jr., how to harmonize. Bandimere Sr. took his love of music a step further when he acquired some studio equipment and used it to record music in his basement. It was yet another example of his diverse interests and multi-dimensional talents.

But in most instances, Bandimere Sr. exercised his leadership behind the scenes. Such was the case in his relationship with Denver Area Youth for Christ. It was 1958 when Jim Groen had just been named director of the outreach ministry. Within a year, the 24-year old minister met and befriended John and Frances at the speed shop on Champa Street. Groen observed how influential Bandimere Sr. was with young people and asked him to be on his Board of Directors.

Together, they developed a program called "Bolts and Bishops" that taught teenage boys how to work on cars. Not surprisingly, Bandimere Sr. opened up his shop for the monthly meetings.

"He loved young people," Groen says. "That was a passion in his life. It was very clear. Young guys that had cars loved to hang around him. He wasn't just selling stuff. He was trying to help guide them through life. John was always right there. He loved those kids. Some of them had deep problems. Some of them were delinquent kids. But their love of cars became a bridge between them and John."

The success of that program carried over into the entire organization that eventually grew to include a staff of nearly 100 people. Denver Area Youth for Christ made its way into the public school system and created a sizeable camp program.

"As a young guy taking over a ministry organization, I didn't know much about what I was doing," Groen says. "I knew I loved young people and wanted to work with young people. John was one of the early board members that gave me counseling. When I had a problem, I felt like I could go to him. I would just go down to the speed shop and we would sit down and talk and he would give me some guidance. I don't know where Denver Area Youth for Christ would be had it not been for my relationship with John Bandimere Sr."

7

We Specialize In Performance

Although John Bandimere Sr. was doing his best to live a more prioritized life, he still had an insatiable passion for performance. His first love was God and family. After that, he loved to work and build and repair. And if he couldn't find the parts he needed, he would invent them.

Yes, his priorities had shifted, but his active mind and constant desire to create and innovate was unchanged if not accelerated.

John the Innovator

Already up to the collar of his trademark coveralls in supercharger technology, Bandimere Sr. faced the continuing challenges that accompanied the burden of being ahead of the curve. General Motors was building blowers that were being used for industrial applications. The 271 blowers, for instance, were used in generators and small diesel engines, while other models were used in war machinery and earth moving equipment.

Using his connections to war surplus following World War II, he worked towards adapting a diesel GM blower to a conventional engine. Bandimere Sr. had to design his own end plates and drives. But he was limited to the V-belts that were available at the time. This problem would be fixed a few years later thanks to the invention of Gilmer belt technology, but in the meantime, Bandimere Sr. was stuck using unreliable technology. The blowers would spin so fast off the crank that the V-belts would break or blow off. It was just another example of Bandimere Sr. being ahead of his time.

Some of his other forward thinking inventions included rocker arm clips that kept the oil from spurting everywhere while adjusting the valves on Chevrolet and Ford V8 engines. Bandimere was also one of the first to make aluminum valve covers. He created a special tool to help mechanics know how much spring pressure there was on the valve springs without taking the heads apart and another tool that adjusted the height of a vehicle.

And in one particular case, Bandimere Sr. came up with a solution to a problem that literally had life-or-death implications. Prior to the 1960s, flywheels were made of cast iron. Under tremendous torque and high RPMs, the flywheels would break apart and at times produced fatal results. At a 1961 race in Scottsbluff, Nebraska, the Bandimere family was on hand when a cast iron flywheel came apart, shot through the floorboard of a race car at the starting line into the timing bus and into the head of the timekeeper who was killed.

Desperate to do something about it, Bandimere Sr. went to Chicago and bought one of the largest lathes available at the time. Using the tool's rotating mechanism, he worked with Mark Williams (now owner of Mark Williams Enterprises, a very successful business that produces racing products) back in the shop on Benton Street to develop the first steel billet flywheel.

"Dad wanted to fix problems," David Bandimere says. "He invented tools to make things less complicated. His mind was always full of ideas to make tasks easier that were usually hard or impossible to do."

For Bandimere Sr., that even meant designing a steam closet that would press clothes without using an iron and what was likely one of the first conceptions of the adjustable bed. And not many from his era can forget the celebrated car polish product known as Wash'nShine.

A 20-dollar job for less than a dime/No more shammies, no more mitts/No more water spots to give you fits

David Beckman remembered that jingle until the very end of his life. Bandimere Sr. had hired Beckman, among other young men, to package and sell the product to dealerships and retail outlets around Denver.

"Night after night, dad had all of these chemicals and he was just relentless," David Bandimere recounts. "He wouldn't go to bed. He was going to come up with a polish that worked the way he thought a car polish should work. He went to such extremes to prove his point. He would brush his teeth with this stuff to prove that he had come up with something that would not only work but that it was safe. It was harmless."

Allan Perotin recalls Bandimere Sr. testing the product on his black 1950 Mercury.

"It was pretty popular for a while," he says. "It would dry to a film and you would just wipe it off and it would take the dirt with it and never scratch the finish."

Bandimere Sr. elicited some impressive endorsements from the likes of General Motors and several of the manufacturer's dealers. David Bandimere still has some of those letters praising the product. The making, packaging, and shipping of the product was a family affair for several years. Bandimere Jr. was the chief mixer of the product and his dedication and hard work earned him a trip to Detroit with Bandimere Sr. to get a brand new 1953 Ford. Wash'nShine was just another example of how Bandimere Sr. used his incredible drive to create unique, unforgettable tools and goods that served the needs of others.

"He trusted in God," Bandimere Jr. says. "He knew God. He understood who God was in his life, and the Lord gave him the answers to all of those problems."

Factory Favor

As his reputation grew beyond the Denver city limits, Bandimere Sr. was able to gain the favor of car manufacturers that were desperately looking for any competitive edge they could find.

In 1957, he traveled with his oldest son to Detroit in his custom GMC Cadillac pickup. En route to a meeting with General Motors executive Ed Cole, the two would routinely be challenged to street races around town.

"It was such fun to be with him when he really let his emotions go wild," Bandimere Jr. says. "I do not remember anyone beating us on that trip."

Cole is often referred to as the father of the V8 Chevy and was

President of Chevrolet during early production of the Corvette. Cole befriended Bandimere Sr. and sold him for only $1 what has become a highly coveted 1957 Chevy Black Widow–a car that would go on to be raced at the Pike's Peak Hill Climb.

"Nobody could beat the factories," David Bandimere says. "They had the money and the engineering. If they could have made it work better, they would have done it. So dad wasn't denying that putting on a supercharger or changing the camshaft or certain kinds of carburetion or injection wouldn't make a difference in performance. But his argument was that if you have a car that you go to work in and drive around town, leave it alone. Tune it up and take good care of it and it will treat you well. But if you want a race car, that's a whole different deal. Don't try to make them the same thing. Don't waste your money on your street car and pretend it's going to be a race car."

Bandimere Sr. was presented with a tailor made opportunity to prove his point that same year. The family was at the shop on Benton Street when a wealthy man from Denver pulled up in a brand new 1957 Mercedes Gull Wing.

"This is the fastest car known to man," he proudly told Bandimere Sr.

More than happy to find out the truth of that bold statement, Bandimere Sr. gathered his wife Frances and youngest son David and headed towards West Alameda Avenue in his supercharged '57 Chevy. He drove to the top of the hill where he left David to determine the winner. From there, the two cars went to the bottom of the hill about a half-mile away. They raced coming back up the hill from a dead stop.

"Dad was at the top of the hill and the Mercedes wasn't even halfway up the hill yet," David recalls. "He must have beat him by a quarter-mile. It was so funny watching this guy try to make excuses. He had spent all of this money on a brand new car. Even for a 12-year old, it was hilarious."

In the early 1960s, his relationship with factories strengthened. In 1961, Bandimere Sr. was the first person west of the Mississippi to receive a 409 Chevy. And it wasn't just one, but two that he obtained. Bandimere Jr. raced with the first one after it was used for the Pikes Peak Hill Climb event while his son-in-law Rich Gager bought the second one and drove it as an everyday car.

From 1962 to 1964, Bandimere Sr. had a contract with Plymouth. They would send him a brand new race-prepped car with 413 and 426 wedge engines that he would test at the Bonneville Salt Flats in northwestern Utah. In one instance, he ran one of these vehicles up to 143 miles per hour.

As he gave the factories invaluable information, they in turn helped him build a reputation as one of Denver's leading figures within the car performance community.

Let's Meet At Bandimere's

Not only was Bandimere Sr. growing a formidable reputation outside of the city, his influence on young car enthusiasts within Denver was also continuing to swell. For most, their first experience was usually at the parts store on 803 Champa Street in downtown Denver.

Harry Lindsay remembers those days well. He was in high school at the time and couldn't wait until he turned 16 and get his drivers license. In 1960, Lindsay was 18 and bought a 1932 Ford three-window coupe that first served as a streetcar but was later converted into a race car.

"A bunch of us guys were hanging out at local drive-in restaurants and cruising up and down the main streets in Denver," he reminisces. "When we got out of high school, the group became bigger and we did a lot more cruising. In the summer and on Saturdays, we would always go down to the Bandimere store, which was an old white house. They had all kinds of parts in there. That was the beginning."

"Let's meet at Bandimere's," someone would inevitably suggest.

From 1960 to about 1962, Lindsay says the store became "the cult place to hang out" during the summers and on the weekends during school. Jake's Auto Parts was across the street, but everyone went to Bandimere.

"It was the place to go," Lindsay adds. "It was more than a hot rod parts store. It was a place to hang out. You met other people there and we were all interested in drag racing."

It was also a place to get some sage advice and quick service.

"I remember going down to the shop on a Saturday and telling

John Sr., that I needed a wiper motor for my '32," Lindsay says. "It had the old vacuum wiper and I needed an electric wiper motor."

"I know exactly where one is," Bandimere Sr. replied.

There were different levels to the store that had been converted from its original function as a house. Lindsay followed Bandimere Sr. to the back and then up a flight of stairs.

"He rummaged around in these shelves for about one minute and then he pulled out a little box with a Bosch motor," Lindsay recalls. "It was perfect. It was a little 12-volt motor. He knew he had it. He probably hadn't looked at it in five years, but he knew exactly where it was."

Lindsay installed the part in his '32 where it continued to function until he finally had to replace it 50 years later.

"That store was like magic," he continues. "It was the golden age. Drag racing was growing. It was a special time. We didn't have a lot of money. We just saved our money and did the best we could. It was a time of great cohesiveness."

Dennis Maurer was among that group. He went on to become the first national champion from Colorado as an F-stock driver. Others included future funny car driver Art Ward and his crew chief Roger Guzman along with Joe Haska, who later ran a car show in Denver, and Larry Montreal, who also had great cars.

Not all of the young men, Lindsay included, went into racing or the car business, but when the opportunity arose, Bandimere Sr. and Frances were never shy about sharing their faith with whomever might walk through the front door.

"There were times when they would pull individual kids aside and sit down and pray for us," Lindsay remembers. "It was odd at the time, but it had a lifetime influence on a lot of us. It also had an effect on us knowing how strongly they felt about going to church on Sundays. That influence helped me become a Christian."

Many from that group, among others, gravitated to the shop behind the house on Benton Street in Wheat Ridge. The typical garage around town wasn't the most wholesome place to hang out. The language was usually rough and pornographic images were commonly in plain sight. But that wasn't the case at Bandimere Sr.'s place. One of the first things patrons saw when entering the shop was an iconic sign that boasted "We Specialize In Performance." But it was another banner with an unusual message that usually caught their eye:

No swearing or foul talk is allowed in this shop. We seek to honor the Lord in this place.

Ron Neff was 22 years old and the proud owner of a brand new 1965 Corvette when he first met Bandimere Sr. at the shop. Although he didn't have a problem with the sign's mandate, one of his friends wasn't so lucky.

"You couldn't say cuss words around him," Neff says. "That didn't bother me, but one of my buddies did say a cuss word and John banned him from coming back for a week. He was quite the guy."

The wholesome environment allowed for Bandimere Sr. to take the role of teacher to his willing students. He understood that they didn't have a lot of money so he wanted to explain basic mechanics and give them an edge when it came to performance and speed. But more importantly, he and Frances treated the young men that came into his shop like family and that made the kind of impression that lasts well beyond the life of an average vehicle.

"We would go over to the house and they'd invite us in for a sandwich," Lindsay says. "They were so inviting to all of us. They treated us like sons. They took us under their wings. Spending time there kept us out of the bars. It made better kids out of us. It gave us pride of ownership. We learned how to clean stuff up and put stuff away. Those are the things we learned by watching. John Sr. taught us to do things the right way."

And Frances' loving touch had just as much impact.

"Frances was like our second mom," Lindsay says. "She was so nice. She'd be working around in the back. You could go around the counter and say hi. She was smart. She knew the business. Everybody respected her. I don't think any of John's success would have happened without her. The whole family worked together and she taught them values. Frances was very special. She was the glue and John was the visionary."

8

The Safety Proving Grounds of America

In the mid-1950s, street racing was rapidly increasing in popularity. Young drivers would rope off roads along locations such as I-25 between Evans and Yale. Sometimes they would even garner the support of local police officers that would create barriers, usually along Alameda Road, to ensure oncoming traffic was diverted from the activity.

Organized drag racing was still in its infant stages. Popularized on the West Coast, the sport spread across the Midwest and gained significant steam on the East Coast, especially in Northeastern states like Massachusetts and New Jersey. Colorado had a couple of drag strips but cruising at the drive-ins like The Frosted Scotchman in north Denver, The White Spot in Englewood, and Berry's in Lakewood was more fun and a great place to pick up a street race. But street racing wasn't completely safe. John Bandimere Sr. knew this and it caused him great concern.

"At that time, there were a lot of street racers," son-in-law Rich Gager recalls. "He wanted a place to get the kids off the street where they could go and race their cars and test them. That's what really motivated him."

John Bandimere Jr. was one of those young guys racing on the street.

"So was my dad," David Bandimere chimes in.

Bandimere Jr. often jokes about how fortunate he and his brother were to have a dad who went with them to go race. But in the back of his energetic mind, Bandimere Sr. was dreaming up a solution or as Jim Taylor describes it, "a gleam in his eye."

Around 1954 and 1955, Bandimere Sr. began promoting the

concept of a facility that would house a drag strip, an oval track and some garages where he could educate young people about auto mechanics and performance. That was his original vision—a place for testing and teaching, and a little bit of racing too. One of his first stops was a visit with a local auto club called the Denver Timing Association. Butch Salter was a part of that group and remembers when Bandimere Sr. made his pitch.

"He wanted to call it the Safety Proving Grounds of America," Salter says. "He was selling lifetime memberships for $25. I was just 16 or 17 years old at the time. Everyone was very interested in seeing if John would succeed."

In 1956, Bandimere Sr. saw an opportunity on his brother Horace's farm that was located off 58th and Ward Road in Arvada. His property had a long valley with a steep hillside and seemed like the perfect location. After going through some hearings, Jefferson Country's three commissioners unanimously voted to pass the zoning for the track. David Bandimere was 11 years old at the time and vividly remembers the mob scene that ensued.

"It was incredibly attended by the families that lived in the area," he says. "At the end of the meeting, dad witnessed the fighting and bickering that was going on between the farmers and the young people."

"We'll show those farmers!" some of them were overheard saying. "We'll go get 'em!"

It broke his heart to do so, but Bandimere Sr. called the commissioners and told them he was withdrawing his zoning request. He didn't want a fight. He wanted to help people.

One of the commissioners was especially moved by Bandimere Sr.'s passion and joined the cause. Over the next several months, he searched the county for a piece of land that would adequately fulfill the vision while alleviating any issues that might arise with farmers or concerned neighbors. He located some ranch property near Morrison that rested in what was then a hidden valley. Bandimere Sr. agreed that it was a suitable location and in the fall of 1957 received a building permit for the land.

"It really taught our family an important biblical principle," Bandimere Jr. says. "God always has the perfect place for you to be."

Hogback Heaven

Geologists define a hogback as a long narrow ridge or series of hills with a narrow crest and steep slopes of nearly equal inclinations on both flanks.

But for Bandimere Sr., the hogback that led up to the Rocky Mountains on the west side of Denver was simply a taste of heaven. He officially purchased a portion of the land in 1958 and immediately began imagining what the valley nestled next to that precipitous backdrop could become.

It's hard to picture now, but at the time, there were three lakes on the property. David Bandimere remembers walking the otherwise barren land with his dad. Bandimere Sr. would tell his son how it would be developed and where he thought the track would go.

"He had the vision right from the beginning," David Bandimere says. "He envisioned the grandstands in the side of the mountain where people could sit and have an incredible vantage point. It was the impossible dream. But dad never lacked the passion and energy. And that came from his passion for the things of God and what he thought God wanted him to do in life. Everywhere he went, he wanted to make a difference for the Lord."

After Bandimere Sr. broke ground, word spread quickly that something exciting was taking place on Rooney Road. Back then, it took 30 to 40 minutes or longer to get to the Morrison location from the family homestead in Wheat Ridge. But that didn't keep enthusiastic hot rodders from showing up to see how they could help.

Longtime friend Bob Janowski recalls helping Bandimere Sr. run water from a spring on the mountain down to the track. Jim Taylor remembers when Bandimere Sr. bought an old road grader and would "push a little dirt around" in the evenings and on the weekends.

In the early 1960s, Mark Williams made frequent trips to do his part.

"Everyone was totally enthused about getting this drag strip running," he says. "For a period of time when I was working with John Sr., I worked with Frank Peterson to put up lights. He bought a bunch of oil well drilling pipe for the light poles and then he bought surplus lighting from the public service company. We drilled holes and put up those lights on our own."

Darrell Zimmerman knew Bandimere Sr. from the auto parts store on 803 Champa Street. He bought speed equipment and resold it at the drag strip in Julesburg, Colorado, where he worked at the time. In 1956, he was appointed NHRA Regional Advisor for the West Central Division and in 1961 became the Division Director. Zimmerman helped Bandimere Sr. with some design concepts in the early stages and watched as he tirelessly worked the land.

"He bought that old Caterpillar and started pushing the mountain out and building the track," he says. "He had very little help. He didn't have any contractors or anything. Of course, he had to hire the asphalt machines to come out and lay the asphalt. But as far as all the leveling and packing of the track and the fencing and the building of the tower was concerned, that was pretty much all John Sr.'s ideas. He was a great individual and a real gentleman."

Near Death in the Valley

Throughout the late 1950s and early 1960s, John Bandimere Jr. was running the parts business with his brother-in-law Rich Gager. Frances Bandimere took care of the books and helped at the store, but John Bandimere Sr. was spending more of his time developing the track.

At the time, Bandimere Jr. and Joanna Gager's expanding families resided in two houses located close to the speed shop on Benton Street. Without a permanent residence and wanting to have more access to the property in Morrison, Bandimere Sr. bought a 60-foot trailer that served as a temporary home for he, his wife Frances and teenage son David.

It wasn't always the safest place to be. Vandals and thieves made frequent visits. Underneath the offices was a basement full of equipment. Despite putting the heaviest locks they could find on the doors, burglars would still break in and steal their goods. And when Bandimere Sr., finally acquired a road grader, he rebuilt the motor back at the shop and began using it at his property.

"The grader had been out there maybe a few weeks and one morning we went out to the track to do some work," David

Bandimere says. "Someone had stolen all the knobs, smashed the battery, broken all the windows and damaged all the gauges on the diesel engine. The vehicle still ran, but that act of vandalism caused the family a lot of heartache."

But it wasn't always humans with whom they had to contend. On many occasions, the region's notoriously wicked windstorms wreaked havoc on the track including one particularly scary incident. Thankfully, the Bandimere family elected not to stay at the track when massive gusts blew through the valley one night and flipped the trailer over.

"I don't think we would have survived," David Bandimere says.

A few weeks later, another storm hit and stripped the trailer down to its frame. The family found parts and pieces of it everywhere. The bathtub was in a nearby field. The sink somehow managed to travel over into Morrison. Their clothes were gone. Nothing was left. And to add insult to injury, it wasn't long after when someone stole the frame. Within a couple of months, the Bandimere's home was non-existent.

In those early days, dangerous power lines and lethal rattlesnakes also lurked throughout the property. But one horrific incident especially testified to the family's precarious existence in the valley. A patient had escaped from a nearby mental hospital and was wandering around the Morrison area. He found his way to a ranch not far from the track where an elderly woman had lived her entire life in a ranch house that dated back to the late 1800s. The mentally unstable man found a hatchet, broke into the house, brutally murdered the woman and cut her into pieces.

It was a snowy night, so it was relatively easy for the authorities to track the man. They followed his footsteps over the hogback and caught him near Red Rocks. The Bandimere family had not gone to the track that night, but the man had been there. Evidence showed that he had walked all around their vacated trailer.

"There's no telling what would have happened if we had been there," David Bandimere says. "That was just one of the many things that have happened over the years that have been nothing less than miracles. God has been so good to us in taking care of what was most important."

Gifts of Kindness and the Great Flood

When Bandimere Sr. first broke ground on the track, he had what his children would later describe as an "I can do it" attitude.

"He just killed himself trying to make it work on his own," David Bandimere says. "It was sad to see what he went through. Day after day, he would come out here and see how people had vandalized things. People would break in and steal things. The heartache was incredible."

Bandimere Sr.'s stubbornness softened as he gradually realized he couldn't do it on his own.

"It is difficult to take a poor private family with one auto parts store and a small manufacturing company and ever pull this off," David Bandimere acknowledged. "God's plan was to bring many wonderful people to help us."

The land was purchased over time in different portions. The first property was bought from a rancher who lived nearby and used the valley to run horses. Bandimere Sr. reached out to his father Fred Bandimere who provided the first source of funding for the purchase of that land. It was a $13,000 loan with a healthy interest rate attached.

"Every week, dad owed his father the interest on that loan," David Bandimere says. "I have quite vivid memories of seeing my grandfather pull up every week and looking for my father and his interest money. Back then acreage could be bought for about $300 an acre so $13,000 was a huge amount of money. To add insult to injury, my grandfather Fred would inform me how foolish my dad was. He would say he is a dreamer with an impossible dream. I wish I had thought to remind him that nothing is impossible if God is in it."

Bandimere Sr. also used money from his manufacturing business that included the sale of his popular rocker arm clips and trademark car polish Wash'nShine, as well as funds from the auto parts store, which was doing well. But the track was sapping the business dry. His sons were struggling to keep it going. Too much money was going into used equipment purchases at area auctions.

In July of 1961, Bandimere Jr. married Lorraine and the two moved into a house on Benton Street. David was a sophomore in high school when he started staying in his brother's old room upstairs in the parts store. He would sleep there at night and then drive to school in the mornings.

One November night that same year, David was upstairs when the gas overhead heater malfunctioned and started a fire. Miraculously awakened from his sleep, he was barely able to breathe with blood coming out of his nose and mouth. He got to the phone and called the fire department, but the flames cut through the line. He didn't know if they had heard his cry for help. As he stood outside his window ready to jump to the concrete patio below, sirens came screaming down the street. The firemen rescued David, but the building was gutted.

"It was a devastating loss," David Bandimere says. "But God used the horrific event to give the parts business a whole new life through the fire sale. It was the financial turnaround that would help make the racetrack possible."

Bandimere Sr. also bartered his mechanical skills for materials and purchased used and sometimes beat up equipment at auctions for small amounts of money. And sometimes he simply received gifts of kindness from people who believed in his dream. Public Service Company of Colorado gave him a variety of helpful items. Bill Coors of the Coors Brewery Company gave him a huge glass line storage tank system that's still sitting up on the hill today.

"The tank provided water for racers to cool their cars," Bandimere Jr. says. "Dad wouldn't take money or sponsorship from Coors because he didn't believe in what they sold. So Bill just gave it to him."

And then there was the Great Flood of 1965. David Bandimere remembers it well. His big brother had flown to California to drive back with him from Biola where he was attending college. That's when Denver experienced one of its worst floods ever along the Platte River. It wiped out bridges, businesses, and families.

One family lost its entire multi-million dollar inventory. Bandimere Sr. found out they were loading the material and taking it to the dump. But he had the trucks diverted to the racetrack and to their yard at the house on Benton Street. David Bandimere hired some high school kids to pressure wash and clean electrical parts all summer.

"It was a miracle of God," he says. "We got thousands of dollars of electrical parts for just cleaning them. Mud and water destroyed certain things but there was a tremendous amount of salvageable parts. I built an entire warehouse in the basement of the building at the track full of this stuff. Those were things God produced for us that allowed us to build the track with very little economic resources."

All along the way, family, friends and inspired community members gave of their time to help Bandimere Sr. turn that impossible dream into a reality.

"In the early days, we had no way to control the mud that came off the mountain during heavy rainstorms," David Bandimere says. "It would constantly mud up the racetrack. Many people were willing to come out and push a broom. It goes on and on—the people that just cared and were there when needed. They did so much out of their love for dad and the family. There was simply no other way we could have done it."

9

Headers and Handicaps

During the late 1950s and early 1960s, development at the track picked up speed. Word continued to spread amongst the car clubs and local street racing scene that something was going on over in Morrison.

But according to Bandimere Sr. employee Mark Williams, there was a lot more wishful thinking than actual belief that a drag strip in their backyard might be a possibility.

"Nobody thought it would get done," Williams says. "Not even the local hot rodders. They never thought it would happen."

That sentiment grew in 1959 when Sid Langston built Continental Divide Raceways (CDR) about 35 miles southeast of Morrison in Castle Rock. The track had big money behind it and featured a 2.8-mile road course, a half-mile oval, and a 4,200-foot drag strip. CDR would quickly gain notoriety after hosting the USAC National Championship and numerous major sports car races.

By 1964, Rocky Mountain Dragway had opened just 25 miles to the northeast in Commerce City. The track in Julesburg was eight years old and almost 200 miles northeast on the Colorado-Wyoming border, but provided yet another option. Both tracks along with CDR represented an increasing amount of competition for a facility that was still three years away from putting together any significant events.

"You wondered why he was going to do all that and if it was going to turn into anything," Harry Lindsay says. "CDR was the place to go. It was a pretty big deal."

Bandimere Sr. would not let the existence of other tracks in the area deter him. Tim Travis experienced that reality first hand.

Travis was a teenager when he started working for his grandfather's company Eaton Metal, but his relationship with the Bandimere family had started a few years earlier when he would hang around the speed shop on Benton Street. Bandimere Sr. worked on his father's 1953 Lincoln and later souped up *his* first car, a 1955 Chevy.

Bandimere Sr. also took care of the company trucks that needed to be tuned up and serviced. His quality work garnered favor from Eaton Metal.

"He was always digging around in our scrap piles," Travis remembers. "John Sr. tried to do everything himself and do it the most inexpensive way. He had a lot of a friends and a lot of energy. And he always wanted to help keep young people safe."

Bandimere Sr. later asked Travis and his girlfriend (who eventually became his wife) to run a concession stand at the track or whatever work needed to be done.

"It was primitive back then," he says. "There was hardly anything out there. It was just a drag strip. The pits were dirt. The approach to the track was dirt. But I loved racing and we didn't have any money so we'd work out there just to be a part of the drags."

Not only did Bandimere Sr., still have a strong desire to get kids off the streets, he also hoped to influence them on a more personal level.

"He wanted to teach them honest, legitimate mechanics," David Bandimere says. "More importantly, he was driven to make a difference on their eternal souls. He knew that those young people needed to know the Lord."

Fence Holes and Fast Cars

Doug Miller doesn't remember how he got into drag racing. He just knows that as a 12-year old growing up in the Denver area, there was a bug in the air and it was contagious.

In 1964, he lived about 12 miles from the Bandimere property in Morrison. While there wasn't much if any formalized racing going on yet, plenty of guys were showing up at the track to rev their engines, take a pass down the track and get some mechanical wisdom from Bandimere Sr.

Miller and his best friend wanted in on the action, so they would tell their parents some made up story about where they were going to ride their bikes and then head straight for the speedway.

"The first time we rode up there, we ended up finding a hole in the fence," Miller recalls. "We would sneak through that hole in the fence. We stood out of the way so we weren't too conspicuous and we'd watch the cars. We thought that was the coolest thing ever."

The boys continued making the trek on a regular basis throughout the summer until one day when they had a fateful encounter.

"We were halfway through the hole in the fence and looked up and there was John Bandimere Sr.," Miller says.

"Aw man, we've had it now," they thought.

"What are you boys doing?" Bandimere Sr. asked.

"We're sneaking in the fence so we can watch the drag races because we don't have any money," they confessed.

To their surprise, Bandimere Sr. let them come on through the hole and never said a word. In fact, he walked with them and sat them down in the old grandstands. For the next couple of years, mysteriously, that hole in the fence never got repaired.

About two years later when Miller was 14 years old, he and his friend arrived at the track through their usual spot in the fence. Bandimere Sr. spotted them from a distance and got their attention.

"Hey you boys!" he hollered.

"Mr. Bandimere never called us by name," Miller says.

He drove up on a road grader and asked a peculiar question.

"Son, can you drive?" he inquired.

"Yes sir, I can," Miller quickly responded.

"Get in that dump truck and move it out of the way for me."

Miller did as he was told. He had learned to drive at an early age and had no problem maneuvering the vehicle as he was asked to do. Later on that day, Bandimere Sr. became curious about something and asked Miller another question.

"How come you boys always ride your bicycles up here?"

"We don't have driver's licenses," Miller truthfully responded.

"But I just asked you to move that truck and you moved it!"

"Well, you asked me to drive, but you didn't ask me if I had a driver's license."

Bandimere Sr. couldn't do anything but laugh.

Later in life, Miller came to understand that Bandimere Sr. knew exactly what he was doing. Even though they thought they were the most special kids in the world, he had probably let other kids in through that fence hole for the very same reason.

"It was like being with your own grandpa," Miller adds. "He was a man of strong faith and that showed through in his kind heart and his goodness to people. We watched him take that track and single-handedly make improvements over the years. He was the guy that would get on the grader and redo the track. We watched him pour his heart and soul into it. That made an impact on me that's lasted my whole life."

Later in life, Miller worked as a truck driver and sales representative for Pennzoil. Over time he rose to an executive position within the company and facilitated vital sponsorships for Bandimere Speedway. Like the track's founding patriarch, he never wanted to seem too important for anyone.

"John Sr. taught me to never get too big to where I forgot to remember the small people," Miller says. "I tried to emulate that my whole life."

Miller never ran a car at the speedway. Neither did Harry Lindsay. But like so many other teenage boys and young men, they loved to watch fast cars in action. Lindsay had been hanging around the Bandimere parts store on 803 Champa Street and the speed shop on Benton Street during the time that the track was under development. Lindsay was in his mid-20s when Bandimere Sr. organized his first official drag race in 1967. Even better was the fact that he was asked to serve as the general manager for that event.

"I was so honored," Lindsay says. "It was unbelievable. We were just kids. We didn't know how everything worked. He had a fellow down on Sheridan Boulevard by Lakeside Amusement Park that actually developed the clocks that we used on that very first drag race. That was the first time I'd ever seen clocks like that. That first drag race was so much fun. I just rounded up a lot of people to help. It was kind of euphoric to see it all come together."

Lindsay and his friends never thought it would become such a historical night. They never imagined that the Safety Proving Grounds of America would become such a successful racing venue years later.

"We did not appreciate what was happening because we couldn't see what it was going to become," Lindsay says. "That was the beauty of the time. We didn't take a lot of pictures back then. We didn't live for the moment because we never thought it would end. You lived it. You didn't try to spend all your time capturing it so you could save the memory. You lived it and it *became* a memory."

Most of the patrons also failed to recognize Bandimere Sr. as a true pioneer until many years later.

"American men will always put a motor in something and compete," Lindsay says. "John Sr. had that vision. He had the foresight to take a piece of dirt on a hillside in Morrison and build a track. And who else would think to do an uphill shutoff area? That added so much safety. He thought of that. He moved a lot of dirt to make that happen."

John Abbott was another of those young men who didn't quite get it at the time.

"At that time and at that age, we enjoyed it and we thought it was a great facility but we just wanted a place to race," he says. "Now that we're all older, we realize that it's one of the best facilities in the United States and probably the best managed."

Abbott knew about the track early on but didn't get out there much until Bandimere Jr. persuaded his father to run dragsters. In hindsight, the lighting was probably not adequate for that first race, but a rainstorm that night made it a moot point. Only two cars out of an eight-car field managed to make it down the track.

It would take much more than bad weather to dampen spirits during this magical time. Much of the camaraderie was birthed out of Bandimere Sr.'s love for young people and his desire to teach them about auto mechanics and performance. The track didn't develop into the training facility as he had hoped, but he still shared knowledge and wisdom with a group of guys huddled around an engine or in countless one-on-one sessions.

"It didn't matter who the young person was, if you walked into his presence and you had a question or you had a problem, he would drop everything to be there for you," David Bandimere says.

That mindset led him to make regular trips during the 1960s and throughout the rest of his life to Warren Tech Career & Technical

High School in Lakewood where he donated all of his old machine equipment and spoke to the engineering classes there.

"His legacy is that he was a teacher," Harry Lindsay says. "He really wanted to help you. Even if his son was competing against you, he wanted to help you. He wanted you to enjoy this wonderful relationship with automobiles."

And for many of those young people, it ultimately boiled down to a greater conversation about spiritual matters and biblical principles.

"I had the highest regard for John Sr.," Tim Travis says. "I loved him very much. We talked often about philosophical things and about family and about Christ. Religion wasn't a particularly important part of my life back then, but he helped make it important. There isn't any young man that had involvement with John Sr., that didn't turn out well. He taught us how to value Christ and how to value others."

Heads Up Headaches

Before 1967, there had been no organized racing at the SPGA but rather a steady stream of grudge matches and test runs. This was partly due to the fact that there were many safety improvements still needed. Among other concerns, there was virtually no lighting, the track wasn't paved all the way, and there wasn't a shutdown area.

That same year, David Bandimere returned home from California with his wife Barbara, whom he had met while attending Biola University. He and a friend from college had moved to Colorado to attend Denver Seminary. Together they devised a punch card system to help generate some money at the track. Racers would come through the gate and buy $1 runs. Admittedly, the system wasn't terribly organized, but it was the best they could do under the limiting circumstances.

They tried other simple things like running a course around the mountain with off-road equipment or racing sports cars on the two-mile oval dirt track that was would later be converted to an access road. In the meantime, Bandimere Jr. and his brother-in-law Rich Gager were holding down the fort at the auto parts business.

After making steady improvements to the facilities, the speedway received sanctioning from the NHRA. This led to a few more events including a heads up program that ran on Saturdays. For several years, there was just one tech inspector and the price to race had steadily increased.

Bruce Tawson and the Sabres Car Club were making money at CDR in Castle Rock with heads up racing. But for a smaller track with virtually no budget, it was almost impossible to keep up. Using the NHRA class rules, cars had to be weighed, cards had to be filled out to identify engine displacement and then cars had to be put into classes based on the size of its engine. If protested, they had to pump the engine to prove that the racer had claimed the correct size. The Bandimere's were losing racers.

"They would have to wait in line and weigh their cars and do all of this displacement stuff with the engine to put everyone in perfect classes," David Bandimere says. "It took so long and it was boring. There had to be another way to make money."

In 1972, Hooker Headers was a popular brand name accessory for many performance-minded drivers in Denver and across the country. Headers were created with the goal of making it easier for the engine to push exhaust gases out of the cylinders. But Bandimere Sr. wasn't sold on the hot item and didn't feel like they made the car run any better. Still, despite telling car owners that they weren't necessary, Bandimere Jr. and his employees at the auto parts store sold thousands of them.

At the time, Hooker Headers was having a national contest to see who could sell the most units of its product. Bandimere Auto Parts was winning until the very end when another store took in a huge order that vaulted them into first place. Instead of winning a brand new Chevy Vega, the Bandimere's took home second prize–a trip for two to attend the NHRA U.S. Nationals in Indianapolis, which is still the organization's longest running event.

John Jr. and David Bandimere took the trip to the Midwest with more than having a good time in mind. They hoped to return with some ideas on how to make the track profitable from someone who was having success. While there, Ira Litchey, who managed the Coca-Cola Funny Car Cavalcade of Stars, helped arrange a meeting for the brothers with his associate Ben Christ in Chicago who was one of the few successful track owners at the time.

"I think that's how God blessed our attitude and our desire to seek wisdom for our business," David Bandimere says. "Ben found in us a couple of guys who weren't gold digging and trying to take advantage of him. He literally took us in like sons. For the several days we were there, it got better and better. He became more open and vulnerable. Ben had brought his top associate with him and spent time with us as we toured his facilities at the US 30 Dragstrip and Lake Geneva Dragstrip where we received some invaluable tips on how to turn a profit in the drag racing world."

Christ introduced the Bandimere's to handicap racing, a system where anyone could be a winner. Here's how it worked:

Drivers would go through time trials. After their run, they would put their time on their windshield with shoe polish. Their times would also be entered into the timing system. When two cars faced off, they would start at different times. The winner was the car that finished first as long as they didn't get a red light on the starting line or if they drove quicker than the time they put on their window, also referred to as "breakout."

The Bandimere's first implemented the new style in 1973, but it wasn't without its complications. For instance, the diehard NHRA fans hated it.

Some drivers would cause trouble by trying to prove the system wrong. They would fly down the track at top speed, then put on their brakes and cross the finish line just ahead of the much slower car. And then there was the racer who, when he would red-light, would literally go as slow as he could as he made his way to the finish line. After numerous warnings, Bandimere Jr. informed him to not return to the speedway.

"We had to weather a lot of contention before we could get people to accept it and work with us on it," David Bandimere says. "But it saved us from the cumbersome inspection lines. It was the salvation of the track."

Over time, the handicap racing program grew to become a successful venture that not only saved the track time and money, but it actually started to turn the financial situation around. This also allowed the Bandimere's to run high school and club events that steadily increased the drag strip's popularity.

The organized High School Drags Program was eventually taken on by John Bandimere III (aka Sporty) and in 2014 celebrated over 25 years of educating high school students the importance of taking their need for speed to a safe, supervised environment.

"The High School Drags Program was unofficially started in the late 1970's when high schools still had Auto Shop classes." Sporty Bandimere explains. "Students from Alameda and Jefferson High School approached my grandpa and asked him if they could organize a race for high school students only and he allowed it. The first year was a bust, but he allowed them to try it a second time and it attracted a surprisingly large group of kids. The High School Drags originally ran on Memorial Day, but then we added an event on Labor Day and also ran it on July 4th for many years. Today, we host the High School Drags on Memorial Day and Labor Day and also have a class for high school students in our E.T. Series. Through our tech inspection process, we make sure that their cars are safe and the kids get the opportunity to hang out with and race police officers."

The Wally Parks Promise

Wally Parks was drag racing's P.T. Barnum. He knew how to put on a good show and he knew how to do it without spending a lot of money. In fact, much of the National Hot Rod Association's early success in the 1950s was paid for with Parks' infectious charisma. He was a very humble and unassuming man with a tremendous passion for the sport of drag racing. As a friend of the Bandimere family, his encouragement provided an important influence in the development of the facility.

Bandimere Sr. first met Parks in 1955 at the NHRA's inaugural national event in Great Bend, Kansas. In the early 1960s, Colorado native Darrell Zimmerman was helping Bandimere Sr. with some early design concepts. He was also keeping Parks informed on progress at the SPGA.

Parks eventually visited the speedway and heard firsthand the vision for what Bandimere Sr. had hoped the place would one day become. At the end of the conversation, he made a bold promise.

"The day will come when this track will host a national NHRA event," Parks said.

After NHRA sanctioned the track in 1968, the Bandimere's started bringing in larger events including the 1973 debut of the High-Altitude Bracketnationals. Local racers were especially excited to see the speedway expand its horizons. In fact, Colorado native and former NHRA Competition Eliminator racer Ron Neff moved to Lakewood in 1968 so he could be closer to the facility.

"When you looked to the left, you'd see that beautiful mountain," Neff reminisces. "When you looked to the right, you'd see the city of Denver. The only thing that was tough was the altitude. Cars didn't perform as good. I had to get used to the differential between Denver and Greeley. But we all adapted to it and learned how to run in the thin air. I hate to use this word so loosely but that place was God's gift to all of us. It really was. There was an incredible camaraderie. And even today, the Bandimere family still treats me like gold."

10

A Family Affair

Former NHRA President Dallas Gardner once told John Bandimere Jr. that owning a racetrack was like owning a gold mine with lots of veins, which, if followed can provide an endless amount of possibilities for operational funding and profit.

"Some of those veins are selling tickets to racers, selling tickets to spectators, selling fuel, selling food, selling souvenirs and selling sponsorships," Bandimere Jr. explains. "Every one of those areas is a vein. Most racetracks have an outside group that handles the sale of fuel, food, souvenirs, etc., and then receives a percentage of the sales. It just made more sense to own and run all of these areas with our own staff."

That has been the case from the very beginning and as the speedway grew throughout the 1970s and 1980s, the Bandimere's worked together to make sure that it ran like a well-oiled engine. It wasn't always the smoothest ride, but the journey ultimately proved that the real gold in that mine wasn't financial success. It was relationships developed with racers, sponsors, NHRA and most importantly, family.

Behind Every Great Man

Long before the speedway hit its stride, the family was forced to face a difficult reality. In 1963, Frances Bandimere had been diagnosed with cancer. Although she continued keeping the books at the auto parts store and stayed active at the track, the next two years were a considerable struggle. She lost her hair from the invasive cobalt treatment and dealt with the typical side effects such as nausea and weakness.

Bandimere Sr. had dreamed of someday providing Frances with

a special house for them to live. Throughout their marriage, they never really had a comfortable place to call home. So when he purchased that first piece of property in Morrison, he finally had his chance. His idea was to build a bungalow at the top of the mountain. It was a breathtaking, exciting concept.

Bandimere Sr., his good friend Ralph Beecher and son David Bandimere, who was 16 years old at the time, worked for months to build a road to the top of the mountain from the valley where the track would eventually reside. David bought cases of dynamite at the feed store in Golden and together they drilled holes and exploded rock.

But Frances become so ill over the last two years of her life that it became impossible for Bandimere Sr. to finish his dream gift for her. During that time, the track, his business and his many projects became secondary. He mostly just wanted to spend time with her.

Frances Bandimere died in November of 1965 at the age of 53. As much as any woman who lived, she exemplified that old cliché: "Behind every great man is a great woman."

"My mother could multi-task," Bandimere Jr. says. "She could do five things at the same time and do them all well. She also had a photogenic memory. She would read her Sunday School lesson one time and then be able to recite it for her class. And she was funny and smart. She graduated from high school when she was just 15 years old."

Tami Shrader has very few memories of her Grandma Bandimere. She was only three years old when Frances passed away. Yet somehow, she is often told that she has many of her grandmother's traits. Not only does Shrader bear a strong resemblance, she also has the ability to multi-task and a nature that allows her to see in people what others don't see and to show them compassion.

"You can be so much like a person but never really know them," Shrader says. "That's almost more than I can handle. That's an emotional thing for me. I know how much my dad loved his mom. For me to have a lot of those traits and not having known her that well, I just think that's a God thing. For some reason, I was blessed with some of her traits. She lives on in our family. It's such an amazing blessing and honor."

And Bandimere Sr.'s love for his wife is yet another inspirational piece of the family history.

"The road that sits on the side of that mountain serves as a monument to Grandma Frances," granddaughter Susan Brown says. "Most people never even notice it, but I do, and when I was a young girl, I dreamed of one day having a man love me enough to build me a road, even if it didn't go anywhere."

All Hands On Deck

There was something about Frances Bandimere's passing that took the fire out of Bandimere Sr. He was still able to do much of the physical work, but it wasn't the same. His dreams were her dreams. They had worked tirelessly as a team to build everything the family had enjoyed up to that point in time. But now that his better half was gone, Bandimere Sr. was lost.

"All of us had to pull together to give dad encouragement so he would still want to work and make things happen," David Bandimere says. "It was a very difficult time. We put in so many hours through the parts business and the manufacturing. We had to make it work."

As the three children's families were growing, David's wife Barbara took over the books along with Russ Hamilton who was hired to help with the businesses finances. David started a surplus store in the building on 803 Champa Street until it was condemned and torn down.

In 1969, Bandimere Sr. became reacquainted with another woman named Frances. She and her husband, also named John, were Gideons and served with the Bandimere's on the Board of Directors for The Heart of Denver, an organization that provided room and board in downtown Denver for young Christian girls that wanted to pursue better jobs. Frances' husband had also passed away. The two widows began dating and were married in 1970.

As the family forged ahead without their beloved matriarch, it quickly became obvious that any successful activity at the speedway was going to require all hands on deck.

Tami Shrader didn't live at the track like her Grandpa and Grandma Bandimere did with her Uncle David back in the late

1950s and early 1960s. It just seemed like she lived there. As a young girl and throughout her teenage years, she and her siblings and cousins could often be found there during the week painting, picking up trash, sweeping, cleaning and fixing things up in preparation for a weekend event.

And while most young people were out with their friends on a Friday or Saturday night, the Bandimere grandkids were having their own unique brand of fun. Except their kind of fun was actually work, and hard work at that.

Over the years, Shrader has, among many other duties, worked at the gate, worked in concessions, and most recently handled community relations. At any given point, if her brother-in-law Larry Crispe were to ask her to run the starting line, she could still do it. Shrader could also, in a pinch, run the ET booth, or sell tickets, or any variety of race day jobs. The same would be true for her sister Johnna Crispe and brother Sporty Bandimere. Regardless of the task and the personnel available, it's all hands on deck at Bandimere Speedway.

"We could do all those things because that's the way we grew up," she explains. "A lot of that came from Grandpa. He wasn't above doing anything. If someone got locked out of his or her car, he would jimmy rig it and get into that car. If somebody needed something in the concession stand, he'd run to the grocery store to get it. I think we learned that from him. Just because you have a title or different areas you excel in, you can still be a part of anything. Whatever needs to be done, you do it."

Shrader's cousin Randy Gager can relate. He and his brother Rick, along with most of his other cousins, took turns working in the ET booth. At that time, the booth was a cylindrical structure made of metal that was about 12 feet in diameter and had a chair and small desk inside. Because the small window provided very little ventilation, the enclosure reached sweltering temperatures during the summer days.

"We would work in pairs and switch off," Gager explains. "One of us would be on the radio communicating with the tower and taking the time and speed and writing it down on cards. The other one would run the cards to the drivers as they came by on the return road. This was where all of us kids learned every cuss word in the

English language, and maybe a few in Spanish, as the drivers would almost always vent their disgust and strong disagreement with the information written on the card. They were just taking out their frustrations on us poor young messengers, but that was a life lesson none of us kids ever forgot."

Gager also encountered some salty language while working at the front gate taking tickets and checking spectators into the facility. No alcohol was sold or allowed on the grounds back then so his fairly innocuous job took on a higher level of difficulty.

"If we discovered smugglers trying to sneak in beer or other alcoholic beverages, we were mandated to confiscate *and* dispose of the alcohol by pouring out each can, bottle, or container," Gager says. "Needless to say, I encountered a few spectators on occasion that were none to happy to have their precious cargo wasted."

When Sporty Bandimere was 12 years old, he was occasionally put in charge of securing the gate that allowed racers and spectators to get from one side of the track to the other. If you didn't have a pit pass, you didn't could go through the gate.

"I would sit up on the wall and I'd open and close the gate and make sure that people had the proper credentials or tickets," he explains. "But you would never put a 12 or 13-year old kid in that position today. Who's going to listen to a kid tell them they can or cannot go beyond a certain point? But I think people's values and respect for others was drastically different back then."

And it wasn't just the grandkids that were needed to take on a variety of responsibilities. John Bandimere Jr., David Bandimere, and David's wife Barbara carried the weight of the day-to-day operations, and their sister Joanna Gager, her husband Rich and John's wife Lorraine were just as invested with their time and energy.

In those early years, the speedway hired people to work the parking lot and others to handle security. The family couldn't pay them much money much less feed them, so Rich and Joanna Gager would work tirelessly to prepare and serve them lunches during a race weekend.

"There aren't many families that would choose the path that we chose," David Bandimere adds. "Everyone played a role. Everyone was critical. If it wasn't for the family members and the people that God brought into our lives, it never could have worked."

The Outlaw Track

Even though the Bandimere track had been sanctioned by NHRA in 1968, that didn't mean the facility was where it needed to be. Much of the concern surrounded what David Bandimere often refers to as the speedway's "strange facilities."

But when Bandimere Sr. first broke ground in Morrison, he had hopes of building the Disney Land of automotives. One of his ideas was to have each building represent a car part. The concept didn't get too far, but it did result in the original tower design being crudely fashioned into the shape of a spark plug.

Tami Shrader has fond memories of that tower. She, along with siblings Johnna and Sporty and cousin Rusty would play all night long in the bed of a pick-up truck at the base of the tower so her mom Lorraine, who was working upstairs, could see them during the races. If the kids got tired, they would lie on the floor of the tower and fall asleep.

"It was a scary building," Shrader says. "You had to walk up a narrow spiral staircase and climb up through a hole to get to the top level. I would always lay right up against the wall next to my mom's feet because I was always afraid that in my sleep I would roll and fall down that hole."

Much to Shrader's amazement, the family added an upper deck to the building and it became a hospitality suite. John Sr.'s brother Horace graciously helped make this possible.

"Back then it worked," she says. "We thought we were so ahead of the game. It wasn't glamorous, but we had it, and we thought it was pretty awesome."

But the sparkplug tower was one of the track's rare amenities. The lighting system was whatever the public service company provided and tickets were sold to spectators through their car windows. For several years, the track also did not have an ambulance or a tow truck. And the only source of water for racers to cool their engines was from a well. It was a reddish orange color due to its iron and sulfur content.

"Early on, there was nothing out there," Shrader says. "It was out in the sticks. We had a straight strip of asphalt. We had a starting line and a finish line. We had a tower. We had grandstands. So we had a racetrack."

The Bandimere family also had many friends that were willing to come out and help run the track that was operating on a bare bones budget. In 1972, a young couple had just moved to Colorado two weeks after getting married. George Abbas and his wife Kathy began attending Beth Eden Baptist Church where David Bandimere was their Sunday School teacher.

By 1974, they had been asked to work at the speedway. Abbas worked in a concession stand his first year and spent the next eight years in the tower announcing over the public address system and helping run the clocks. Abbas, who previously traveled as a music minister with his wife, is now a pastor at Columbine Baptist Church in Littleton. But back then he also took on an impromptu role as one of the track's chief hunters. Wild animals would routinely run onto the strip and cause racers to swerve to avoid a violent hit.

"They just hated it when they hit a rabbit at 130 miles an hour," Abbas says. We did what we could to keep the population down and the racers safe."

The unique layout and the barely functional facilities were at times the least of the family's worries. Until about 1987, David Bandimere says the speedway was "the classic outlaw track."

"We attracted a fairly rough crowd," he says. "There were a lot of people who took great pride in their race vehicles, whether it was a motorcycle or a car. They typically came in a group and didn't want to be told to follow the rules. We were trying to create a safe environment, but it was difficult to do without their respect."

David Bandimere experienced some of the scariest moments firsthand. One night, about 40 people came over the hill out of the dark and rushed into the facility without paying. On another occasion, he had apprehended two intoxicated men who had tried to sneak in, but they quickly turned the tables and put a knife to his throat in the dark parking lot.

Proverbs 15:1 came to his mind in that moment.

"A soft word turns away anger."

Taking King Solomon's words to heart, it was a calm, gentle response that saved his life.

"It was survival," David Bandimere says. "People parked everywhere and snuck in everywhere. You just did what you had to do to survive. That's what we really lived. We didn't have the money to fence things in and the right infrastructure to handle traffic. So we just did the best we could do."

And just like his teenage days staying at the track with his parents, there was still a steady flow of vandalism. It got so bad that family members would take turns keeping watch. When David and his wife Barbara were newly married, they often slept in the tower at night. It wasn't uncommon for people to drive up to the track on motorcycles and bust through the fence.

Several years later, Sporty Bandimere and Larry Crispe approached some guys that were causing trouble and told them to leave. After shutting down the facility, Sporty was outside of the office building and noticed that the men were still there. After again telling them to go home, one of the troublemakers took a cheap shot and hit Sporty square in the nose. Blood went everywhere. His older sister knew that at times this business could be risky, but putting themselves in danger like this sometimes made her question if it was really worth it.

Despite the strange facilities and dicey situations that sometimes arose at the so-called "outlaw track," there was mostly a lot of family fun as the speedway went through its early stages of growth. According to Abbas, that often meant getting in on the action.

"As it would get late in the evening, we would wait for the last few cars to cool so they would make their last round," he says. "Every once in a while, we would go down there and run our vehicles just for the fun of it. We'd make a quick pass or two and then go back to work."

And the younger grandkids that weren't old enough to work yet found all kinds of things to do on the vast property. Susan and Skip Bandimere, for instance, would take the racers' kids on tours through the drainage system.

"We would just run around and cause trouble and climb up the mountain," Sporty Bandimere adds. "There was a huge boulder that rolled down the side of the mountain and ended up landing next to the return road. It was kind of concave and we'd sit up on that rock and watch the races from there. That rock was there for years."

Because there were no residents nearby, sometimes those nights would last until two or three in the morning. On some occasions, the family would leave the track and stop to have breakfast before going home and getting into bed.

"Things were pretty simple," Sporty Bandimere adds. "It was a lot of fun. Everybody knew each other. We knew all the racers' kids. You could run around and have a good time."

Confessions from the Concessions

Sometimes work and fun came together in the most unusual places. Perhaps not surprisingly, that unlikely combination involved food, or at least the business of selling snacks and carbonated beverages to the speedway's hungry and thirsty patrons. While the concessions stands provided an opportunity for the track to turn a profit, they at times were merely playgrounds where the grandkids could have a good time.

When Lorraine Bandimere ran a concession stand, she would take her daughters Tami and Johnna every Friday afternoon down to Star Bread Bakery in Denver and load up the family Suburban with hot dog buns and hamburger buns.

"Johnna and I would always have to open up one of those bags and eat a fresh hot dog bun," Tami Shrader says. "It smelled so good and mom would say, 'Okay, you can have *one* hot dog bun.' They were so soft and so awesome."

As each kid got old to enough to run his or her stand, Lorraine Bandimere would give her kids this odd piece of instruction:

"Go ahead and eat as many hot dogs, hamburgers and candy bars as you want," she said. *"And drink as much pop as you want."*

And they did just that until they no longer cared to see another hot dog, hamburger, candy bar or cup of soda again.

"It actually worked in her favor," Shrader says. "We got our fill of it and eventually we got to the point where we didn't even like that stuff anymore."

Of course, it wasn't always fun and games. When the track first opened, Joanna Gager ran the concession stand out of a small trailer. It was difficult to secure the product that was stored inside, especially with so much wildlife running rampant.

"We would come back on a Friday after closing things up the previous weekend and find that mice had destroyed entire boxes of candy bars," Shrader recalls. "We hated it when that happened, but we had to deal with it. We had to clean up the mess and sanitize the entire trailer before we could open things back up."

And then there was the infamous popcorn fire.

Due to the track's shoestring budget, the family often bought used equipment from other tracks that had gone out of business. But that also meant they sometimes inherited their problems.

Shrader's concession stand had such a piece of equipment. It was an old popcorn maker that had an open flame that cooked the kernels. At the time, a man named Harry Tipton was in charge of concessions. If the popcorn ever caught fire, he had instructed the workers to take the scooper and pat it out. Then they could simply scoop out the burnt popcorn.

"On this particular night, we were open for business and sure enough the popcorn caught on fire," Shrader says. "We were calmly patting it out with the scooper when all of the sudden, I hear a commotion behind me."

"Get out of the way! Fire!"

Here came Harry Tipton flying through the door wielding a fire extinguisher. As he overzealously sprayed foam at the popcorn machine, he slipped on the floor, wet from the leaking ice machine, and fell right on his back in the middle of the concession stand. What a mess it was. They were in the middle of a big race, and now Shrader had to clean up the yellow extinguisher foam that covered everything while still trying to take care of hungry customers.

"There sure were a lot of hijinx in the concessions stands," she admits. "We learned a lot in the early days and after hiring Paul Lombardi to manage the food service 25 years ago, Bandimere Concessions has become its own business at the track."

The Sunday Solution

As the track took on more events, the challenges that accompanied the running of night races intensified. Due to his job overseeing public safety, David Bandimere was especially feeling the heat.

"A lot of people were being sent to detox," he remembers. "They were sneaking in beer and who knows what else. There were huge fights and people were getting hurt. There was something about the darkness that brought out the worst in people."

In 1984, John Bandimere Jr. confronted his father in the office basement. He saw what his brother was going through and knew a change had to take place.

"Why would you build a place like this that you can't run on Sundays?" Bandimere Jr. frustratingly asked.

"I understood why we didn't run on Sundays," he explains. "I knew about my dad's personal convictions. But I didn't understand why he would build a track when you couldn't utilize it on the days when people were most likely to come."

Soon thereafter, the conversation led to a fateful meeting between father and son in the speedway conference room. Sitting at opposite ends of the table, he laid a large cluster of keys and pushed them across to Bandimere Jr.

"It's not mine to run anymore," he said. "It's yours."

The next season, Bandimere Speedway was no longer forced to race late into the night on Saturdays. Instead, races finished at a reasonable hour with the finals concluding in broad daylight on Sundays.

"Dad was really disappointed in us at first, but it wasn't because he was going to be embarrassed or that we were dishonoring the Lord," David Bandimere explains. "He was fearful that Johnny and I would end up doing what he did and get so involved in the racing business that we would start to neglect our families."

Bandimere Jr. and his brother have worked diligently to try and make sure that didn't happen, however the business they are in has a tendency to make it hard to have a balanced set of priorities that centers around their faith in God and their devotion to family.

"We have not become complacent," Shrader says. "The race-track definitely belongs to God. That was the way my grandpa would have wanted it. Every Sunday that we have a race during the summer, we have a chapel service. Because we have a place where people are spending their time on Sundays, it's important to our family that we honor it. We remind people that it's Sunday and honor the fact that it's Sunday.

When the family started racing on Sundays, there was a noticeable difference when those late night races were brought into the light.

"It was just peaceful," David Bandimere says. "It was calm. That was the thing we were having a hard time making our dad understand. We either needed to give it all up or we had to go to a Sunday final for the national event."

Throughout 1984 and until his second wife's passing in April of 1985, Bandimere Sr. wasn't able to come out to the track as often as he once did. But every once in a while, on a Sunday no less, Bandimere Sr. would drive Frances out to the track and park by the tower. He was curious about how things were going.

"You could tell he didn't quite want to let things go," granddaughter Johnna Crispe notes. "It was still his baby. He wanted to make sure things were still running the way he wanted them to run. Even today, we're still trying to finish what he started. We're still trying to keep kids off the street. We're trying to establish a safe place for people to experience speed in their cars. It is what he would have wanted it to be. We're doing everything in our power to keep his dream alive."

Bandimere Auto Parts ©
DENVER

11

Cavalcade of Stars

Throughout much of the 1970s and into the mid-1980s, the Safety Proving Grounds of America, or SPGA as it was still called back then, added divisional races and slowly gained some much needed momentum with drag racing fans in the Denver area. The family also took out a loan to install grandstands and to fund surface improvements.

The Bandimere's created new races like the popular Nitro Knockout that featured top fuel dragsters and hosted touring events such as the Coca-Cola Funny Car Cavalcade of Stars, a circuit event that wasn't a national points event but rather a match race exhibition.

But the track still struggled to get press from the local sports media who at the time was much more interested in covering professional and college sports teams like the Denver Broncos, the Denver Nuggets, and the University of Colorado football program. Motorsports didn't get much respect or coverage no matter what was going on.

To remedy the problem, the speedway began hosting an annual media day at the track. Reporters would tour the facility, meet with drivers and take spins down the track. The tide slowly turned in the Bandimere's favor, but not without a healthy dose of hard work, creativity and personal touch.

Pressing the Flesh

Attracting press to cover events at the track was a consistent challenge. It was clearly time to step up its marketing and publicity efforts. In 1975, the Bandimere family met a young man who would help on both fronts.

Steve Ciancio first encountered the family through the auto parts store while in high school. The facility in Morrison was still being developed as he attended the University of Colorado at Denver in pursuit of a journalism degree with an emphasis in advertising. His original intent was to write for one of the major racing publications.

Some of his early freelance work began at Rocky Mountain Dragway where he took his own camera and started taking pictures. While there, he met a man with Speed Journal who hired him to cover the local drag racing scene. That led him to Bandimere Speedway where he formally met Bandimere Jr., and covered the track's events for National Dragster.

From 1975 to 1976, Ciancio continued to cover the sport on the side while working at the Denver Post. Then in 1977, Bandimere Jr. hired him as the speedway's first marketing director. His job also included advertising and sponsorship development.

"When I joined the staff at the race track, John Jr. had just started some major spectator events," Ciancio recalls. "Prior to that, it had mostly been bracket racing on Friday and Saturday nights for a long time. The local drivers were racing a lot of late '60s and early '70s muscle cars like Chevelles and Mustangs and GTOs."

When he first arrived, the track offices were in downtown Denver, but they eventually moved to a small building complex on the east side of the facility. Although Bandimere Jr. was starting to take a more prominent leadership role, Bandimere Sr. was still around and continuing to make lasting impressions.

"He was a really neat guy," Ciancio fondly remembers. "He was the inventor or the mad scientist in his laboratory. He had so much passion. Whatever he was working on, he actually threw himself into it. He could work around the clock without eating or sleeping if he was working on something that he was really into. He was quite a character. I really enjoyed being around him."

Ciancio worked closely with Bandimere Jr. for nine years. Over that time, he grew to appreciate his boss's outgoing personality and engaging charm.

"John Jr. is an impressive figure in the community," Ciancio says. "Back in those days, drag racing was generally viewed by the community as something they did on the streets and something that would get you a ticket from the cops. Drag racers were thought to be the guys in the black T-shirts. They had grease under the fingernails. Some of the guys had sketchy character. They weren't looked upon very favorably. But here came a guy in John Bandimere Jr. who was a clean, wholesome, professional family man and a member of the business community. He put a different face on drag racing in Denver."

Ciancio also recalls long hours in the office like those instances when he would stay until midnight laying out the track's promotional magazine, The Elapsed Times. He would be back the next morning at eight o'clock working on another project. Sometimes the routine was seven days a week. The hard work often took a physical toll including one comical instance at the Mile-High NHRA Nationals.

"We had a press day with all the drivers and writers at Malibu Grand Prix," Ciancio says. "As a thank you for letting them use the facility for our press day, we brought some of their cars and drove them up and down the drag strip during the opening ceremonies. Back in those days, the finals were still on Saturday night. John Jr. had been busting his tail to get the track ready for primetime and he was driving one of the cars. As the announcer was introducing the dignitaries and we were getting ready for the national anthem and other opening ceremonial events, the staff looked over and saw John sound asleep in the car. He winked out right there with 25,000 people in the grandstands right before the signature event of the year."

While the local media was important to the track's growth, Bandimere Jr. was also interested in developing better relationships with potential sponsors. Ironically, it was a kid who used to sneak in through the fence hole that became one of the speedway's most valued partners.

In the late 1960s, Doug Miller started working for Pennzoil as a delivery driver and salesman in the Denver area. The Bandimere family bought oil from Miller for their auto parts shops. Miller later became a regional manager and traded Bandimere Jr. cases of oil to give to the bracket winners in exchange for sponsorship.

During those early days, the track utilized an oil tank on wheels that was filled with water for the racers to cool down their radiators. Miller wanted to expand Pennzoil's presence at the track but didn't have a budget to do so. He presented Bandimere Jr. with the idea of naming the water tank the "Pennzoil Water Tank." The track announcers would reference it that way over the public address system and tell racers where it would be located. Once a year, Miller and some of his workers would sand it down, prime it, and paint it with the Pennzoil logo.

Over time, Pennzoil became more sophisticated in its advertising and marketing within the drag racing world. Miller purchased a fifth-wheel trailer and decorated it with its trademark logo that featured a likeness of the Liberty Bell. He called the unit the "Pennzoil Bell." It would travel around the country to race events and would host customers and drivers and facilitate autograph sessions.

"Because I had such a great relationship with John Jr., we were the sole oil sponsor at Bandimere Speedway," Miller says. "He would always give us a prominent place to park that trailer and give us a lot of visibility."

But for Bandimere Jr., pressing the flesh wasn't always about garnering media attention or signing corporations and local businesses to long-term sponsorship deals. It was about being a consistent presence in the lives of everyone he encountered at the track whether that might be a reporter, an entrepreneur, a fan or a racer and their family.

Dave Jackson fit three of those four descriptions. He started attending races in the mid-70s and got the racing bug in the early 1980s and regularly competed in the King Street and Pro Mod divisions. Jackson also opened his own insurance company and assisted the Bandimere family with its coverage needs. He, like so many others, experienced their love for people and their passion for the sport.

"I got to know them because of their kindness," Jackson says. "The family would just walk around and get to know people. We'd cook hamburgers and we'd invite John to come by and he would take time out to do that. As a racer, I'd ask John to lead us in a prayer for the day. He loved to do that and it gave us such a comfort."

Bullets and Rockets

During the late 1960s and through much of the 1970s, stuntmen and daredevils were all the rage. Evel Knievel was famous for his leg-

John Bandimere Sr. (left) and Bill Vincent (right) with one of Colorado's first known snowmobiles that John Sr. built in 1936.

John Sr.'s first auto shop in Denver, Colorado, at 14th & Broadway in 1938.

(from left to right) David Beckman, Bill Vincent and John Bandimere Sr. with the Sheridan Evangelical Church Sunday School class in 1943.

David Beckman at the Bandimere Benton Street garage in 1942.

The Bandimere supercharged 6-cylinder demonstrator and delivery truck with a photo of the engine that was in the truck.

John Sr. at a street race on the east side of Denver, Colorado.

John Sr. with his original 1949 GMC Truck before its conversion to a GMC Cadillac.

John Sr. and Frances Bandimere – a true love story.

John Jr., Betty Vincent and Allan Perotin in 1949.

John Sr. in his Pikes Peak car in front of the parts store on 803 Champa Street.

John Sr. (left) leans in to talk to his driver Hugh Thomas (right) at the Pikes Peak Hill Climb in the early 1950s.

Frances Bandimere spending time with Hugh Thomas' wife Janelle at the Pikes Peak Hill Climb in the early 1950s.

The first 409 Chevrolet with 360-horsepower to come to Denver, running the Pikes Peak Hill Climb. John Jr. would later street race this car.

The Bandimere Family in the early 1950s: (left to right) John Jr., David, Frances, John Sr., and Joanna.

John Sr. and his supercharged Cadillac roadster as onlookers await a Thanksgiving street race at Ridge Road on November 22, 1951. (Photo credit: Vern Raymer)

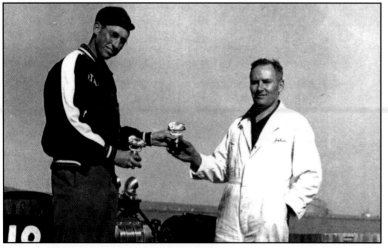

John Sr. receiving a trophy from Jim McKindley, president of the Denver Timing Association, after his win against Kenz & Leslie on Thanksgiving Day in 1951. (Photo courtesy of the Jim McKindley collection)

John Sr.'s '55 Chevy being towed to the starting line by his GMC Cadillac Truck at the first NHRA national event held in Great Bend, Kansas, in 1955.

John Sr.'s self-built V-16 Chevrolet motor. This prototype never ran.

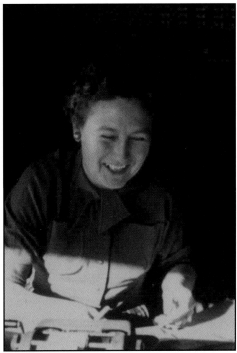

A 1955 article in the Denver Post newspaper featuring John Sr. (far left) and his advocacy for safer street racing. The photo was taken in the backyard of the Bandimere house on Benton Street. John Jr. far right.

Frances Bandimere sitting behind her desk at the parts store on 803 Champa Street.

John Sr. with a reporter from Hot Rod Magazine checking out a supercharged engine he installed.

John Sr. displaying some of his inventions during a major auto show at the Denver Coliseum.

John Sr.'s 1955 Chevy and drag racing's first semi-truck hauler at the NHRA national event in Great Bend, Kansas.

John Sr. racing at the Salt Flats in a car that David Bandimere would later drive to Biola University in California.

John Sr. with his 1955 Chevy at the NHRA national event in Great Bend, Kansas. Notice the famous black box supercharger from McCulloch.

A label for John Sr.'s famous Wash'nShine car polish. John Sr. even used his musical ability to compose a jingle (song) about the polish.

NEW ALL-PURPOSE WASH'N SHINE

The Amazing Combination Wash and Polish *for car and Home* with BUILT-IN PROTECTION

Recommended by:

John Sr. with his supercharged 1956 Chevy. This car ran on pump gas and could also switch to an alcohol system. Very fun to drive!

John Sr.'s Black Widow 1957 Chevy in action at the Pikes Peak Hill Climb. Chevrolet sold him the car for $1.00.

John Sr.'s winning car at the Pikes Peak Hill Climb driven by Frank Sanborn with a Mopar Hemi engine. John Sr. and Tommy Bricker had to build special main bearing locks to keep them from turning which was the trick that allowed the win.

John Jr. (left) and John Sr. (right) behind the counter at the parts store or 803 Champa Street.

John Sr. on an earthmover during early construction of the Safety Proving Grounds of America.

John Sr., Tommy Bricker and Frank Peterson working construction on the track's first tower.

An early SPGA promotional flier for the Night Drags.

John Sr. in "Grandpa's Toy," a Renault 16 race car with a supercharged Chevy engine.

An aerial shot of the track layout in the early 1960s.

John Sr. (center), David to his right and John Jr. (second from left) with the crew at a drag race in Scottsbluff, Nebraska during the early 1960s.

John Jr. and Lorraine Bandimere constructing the east side grandstands during the 1970s.

View from the staging lanes as cars make runs on the racetrack in an attempt to dry it after a rainstorm.

Early racing at Bandimere Speedway in the mid-1980s.

View of the starting line from the west side concrete grandstands during the mid-1980s.

(Left to right) "Big Daddy" Don Garlits, John Jr., and "Miss Mighty Mopar" Judy Lilly at the 2008 Mopar Mile-High NHRA Nationals.

(Left to right) David Bandimere, Joanna Gager (Bandimere) and John Bandimere Jr. standing in front of the commemorative John Sr. Blvd. street sign on the starting line at Bandimere Speedway. (Photo credit: Scott Arnold)

(Left to right) Larry Crispe, John Bandimere Jr. and John Bandimere III (Sporty). (Photo credit: Scott Arnold)

Matt Hagan and his Mopar-sponsored Funny Car at the 2013 Mopar Mile-High NHRA Nationals. (Photo credit: Traction Twins)

John Force and John Bandimere Jr. at the 2013 Mopar Mile-High NHRA Nationals.

John III (Sporty) Bandimere's 1955 Chevy that has the famous black box supercharger.

Mike Edwards and his Pro Stock car sponsored by Penhall, K&N, Interstate Batteries and I Am Second at the 2013 Mopar Mile-High NHRA Nationals. (Photo credit: Traction Twins)

endary jumps while actor Steve McQueen became known for per-forming his own car stunts. Even failed attempts from the likes of Kenny Powers captured the imaginations of thrill-seekers across the United States.

This provided a unique opportunity for drag strips like Bandimere Speedway. Enter Bullet Bailey. During the mid to late 1970s, this ambitious stuntman put titanium pads on his knees and elbows and would then be pulled down a racetrack at 200 miles per hour. Local businessman and former Jolly Rancher president Bob Harmsen talked Bandimere Jr. into paying Bailey his $1,500 fee to perform the stunt at the track.

"We had an alcohol funny car pull him down the race track," Harmsen recalls. "The guy driving down the track didn't know if he was going 180 or 200. He got up to speed and then started slowing down. That's when Bullet came very close to sliding underneath the car. Before that happened, the driver sped up again. When Bullet let go, he went up the hill. John retrieved him at the end of the track and put him in the back of a truck. Amazingly, he wasn't hurt. He was shaken up a little bit, but we decided not to do that again."

The subsequent arrival of rocket cars further fueled the American speed community's fire. These futuristic looking vehicles ran on hydrogen peroxide and reached unprecedented rates of velocity.

"They didn't make any noise," Sporty Bandimere says. "But they went incredibly fast."

In the late 1970s and early 1980s, Kitty O'Neill created a stir with her notable work as a stuntwoman and rocket car driver. O'Neill was deaf but was able to read lips well. In 1977, she piloted a rocket car to a record-breaking quarter-mile elapsed time of 3.22 seconds at 396 miles per hour, and during another run topped 412 miles per hour.

When she came to Morrison for an exhibition at Bandimere Speedway, she made two runs at 336 miles per hour, which nearly ran her car off the end of the track.

"Today, we've got top fuel cars running 320 to maybe just under 330 miles per hour in 1,000 feet," Sporty Bandimere adds. "But back in the '80s, these rocket cars were going over 330 miles in a quarter mile. It was an unbelievable thing to see."

A few years later, Tim Perry brought a funny car that was powered by one of Bill Fredericks' rocket engines. He called Bandimere Jr. and told him was going to make a run under five seconds. During the mid 1980s, that would have been very impressive.

Perry had only made a few runs elsewhere before showing up in Morrison and managed to put down a blazingly quick 5.01 ET. But unfortunately, one of his crewmembers inadvertently forgot to pull the safety pins out of the parachute packs before the run. When Perry hit the parachute lever, the chutes didn't deploy and he violently crashed his car at the end of track.

Tami Shrader remembers the speedway's refurbished ambulance they called "The Ghostbuster" racing down the track to the scene. Perry was whisked away to the St. Anthony's Hospital where he was covered in salve but before the hydrogen peroxide was washed off. The acidic cocktail ate into his skin and left severe burns on his legs. Although it initially looked as if Perry might not make it, he did manage to survive the horrific incident.

It wasn't long after that when drag racing officials made rocket cars illegal, although they still continue to be run in other countries. The cars were simply too much of a risk.

"When you light a rocket, you can't shut it off," Sporty Bandimere explains. "Once its lit, it's lit. So they had to measure the fuel consumption of these vehicles perfectly so it would run out in that quarter mile. If the rocket stayed lit any longer, it wasn't going to stop. Because of that, there was a certain element of danger every time they were out on the track. But boy were they cool to watch."

Coming of Age

As the speedway increased its schedule, more prominent figures within the drag racing world were showing up in Denver and the local racers were getting more serious about protecting their turf. That meant pushing the limits of mechanical engineering in order to beat the tricky altitude.

Former NHRA Competition Eliminator racer Ron Neff was originally from Greeley, Colorado, but relocated to Lakewood so he could call the drag strip in Morrison his home track. He saw the thin air as an opportunity to silence the naysayers.

"There was a correction for any track that was over 1,000 feet altitude," Neff says. "You could run an 8.0 at Bandimere Speedway, but it would be corrected to 7.55. So if you set a record in Denver, people across the country would say, 'Well, you can't go that fast at sea level!' We loved to go to sea level to prove them wrong and run better, like the one year where we set the national record four times at four different tracks."

Eddie Hill wasn't from Colorado, but he certainly felt at home in the Rockies. Since 1955, Hill had been racing land dragsters, motorcycles and top fuel boats. In 1985, the Texan decided to get back into drag racing. After his first 15 races, he finally got out of the first round and made his first final in the same weekend. It just so happened that Hill's breakthrough took place at the 1986 Mile-High NHRA Nationals.

"We were running really good up until the final," Hill recalls. "Our engine was still running good but unfortunately we had a bearing separate in the reversing mechanism that we use to backup after the burnout. The car wouldn't back up. We had some of our competitors run out on to the track to push our car back to the starting line. Scott Kalitta came out and got on the front of the car and was pushing it back so we could run the final. I kept trying to engage reverse so I could get back in time. Each time I would try to put it in reverse, the car would stop suddenly. One time, Scott fell on the front of the car when it stopped and skinned his knees."

Hill's opponent was Larry Minor. He waited patiently at the starting line and even elected to not stage his car until Hill was ready to race.

"He didn't have to give us that much time," Hill says. "Finally, when he realized we weren't going to make it, he reluctantly went ahead and ran. He only made two final rounds in his career and he got booed at this one because the fans thought he was taking advantage of my mechanical problems. But he waited way longer than he should have."

After the run, Hill went over to thank Minor for being such a gentleman.

"I remember he looked at me with great apprehension as I was walking up," Hill says. "I guess he thought I was going to voice my displeasure for not waiting longer, but in fact I was going over to thank him for waiting so long. He waited so long he hurt his engine."

Hill has raced all over the country and has won trophies in each of the last eight decades. He is the only racer to win the Top Fuel Championship on both land and water. But Hill admittedly has a special spot in his heart for Bandimere Speedway.

"It's a very memorable place," he says. "Out of all the places we go, that's always a place where we try to get there early and stay there late and try to do some site seeing. Denver is such a beautiful place. We really enjoy our time up there. It's a very special place."

And the racing is sometimes just as unique as the mountainous backdrop.

"Bandimere Speedway was the only place where I couldn't tell if the parachutes had popped at the end of the run," Hill says. "I'd pull the shoots and I couldn't feel them hit. I started using the wheel brakes because I wasn't absolutely sure if the parachutes were deployed and slowing me down or not. In all the other places we've raced, you can definitely tell when the chutes deploy. It's like a big hand reaching out and grabbing you. But up there in the high altitude, you can't feel it."

Like the Bandimere family, Hill and his wife Ercie are also ardent supporters of the Racers For Christ ministry. Both of them have been honored as RFC's Person of the Year on separate occasions. Because of their Christian faith, they have found a bond in Denver that goes well beyond the racetrack.

"When you're running a Top Fuel car, you don't have much time to socialize," Hill explains. "But we did make it a point to go to the Racers For Christ church service every Sunday morning early before the races. We have always been impressed by their faith and their morals and their ethical commitment. We feel like they are kindred spirits."

As the track's profile rose thanks to great performances from the likes of Neff, Hill and legendary drivers such as Don "The Snake" Prudhomme and Tom "The Mongoose" McEwen, the Bandimere family could feel that a momentum shift was taking place in their favor.

"It felt like the track was coming of age," Sporty Bandimere says. "It felt like we were finally arriving as a facility."

Brute Force

In 1978, a relatively unknown driver came over the mountain and saw the city of Denver in all of its snow-covered glory. John "Brute" Force (as he used to be called) was from a Los Angeles sub-urb and, outside of a handful of visits to Arizona, Washington and Oregon, had rarely been much further to the east. And the only snow the 29-year old had ever seen was in Big Bear up in Northern California.

"This is over," he immediately thought. "How am I gonna' get back home?"

Fresh off his sponsorship deal with Wendy's, he was heading to Bandimere Speedway for a match race that marketing representative Linda Tegtmeier had arranged. But Force knew all too well what would happen if the event was cancelled.

"If you don't get a paycheck, you don't have gas money and you can't get home," he says. "You're locked in your hotel room until dad sends you some cash."

Force has come a long way since those days when he was most-ly known as a leaker (a driver who leaked oil all over the track) and the guy who performed extended burnouts at the starting line in an effort to get the fans on his side. Each day spent in his team shop he can see a prominently hung picture that captures the first time he met the Bandimere's.

"John Bandimere Jr. told me it was going to be okay," Force recalls. "It was Colorado. The snow was no big deal. Everything would be fine. And he was right. We packed the place and I met a real unique family."

That trip to Denver turned out to be even more eventful than Force could have imagined. At the time, he was winless in NHRA competition. There wasn't much interest from the media. But Bandimere Jr. took him to meet with Scott Stocker from the now defunct *Rocky Mountain News* for an interview. Force has since become legendary for his ability to talk on camera and tell stories, but this was a big deal.

"Somebody was actually going to sit down and interview me," Force says. "I remember going to one of those stainless steel cafes they've got in Denver, one of those old diners. I went in there and this guy did a whole story. We sat around all day and all night and waited for the story to come out. We waited at the newsstand so we could read our names in the paper. John Jr. didn't realize the importance of that. Most of the big names like Prudhomme and Garlits took it for granted. But to me it was something."

Bandimere Jr. also introduced Force to Jolly Rancher CEO Bob Harmsen. As a prominent motorsports sponsor, he worked with the likes of NHRA drivers John Abbott and Don Garlits and even some NASCAR drivers like Mark Martin. But nothing could prepare him for the day John Force walked into his office.

"I didn't think I was ever going to get rid of him," Harmsen says.

"I need a sponsor," Force bluntly stated. "I'll take anything you can give."

"Here's a check," Harmsen responded as he quickly scribbled out a modest dollar figure. "Now get out of my office."

That relationship ended up lasting for 15 years although it took a while for it to produce results.

"I used to go out to the races with him and I just hoped he would qualify," Harmsen says.

The candy entrepreneur also remembers a comical incident when he went to California for a meeting. Force didn't have much money at the time. He was racing from city to city to pay the bills. When he picked Harmsen up from the airport, he somehow managed to show up in a limousine. But the charade was exposed when he escorted his sponsor back a few days later in an old beat up Volkswagen.

"In those early days, I didn't have an office," Force says. "My wife and I worked out of the house. She was going to college. In the midst of it, my dad took the calls at home and then he'd call me. I traveled on his credit card when I ran out of money because some promoter didn't pay me. In my career, most of the promoters were pretty good to me. But John Jr. was the best. If you ask any racer about any track where they've raced, somebody will have a complaint about how something went wrong, but I don't think you'll ever hear that about the Bandimere family."

12
Lessons from Grandpa

John Bandimere Sr. didn't always put his family first. Prior to his Sunday racing sabbatical, he struggled to find the right balance between work, family and spiritual discipline. But once his grandchildren came along, his priorities had radically changed even though his drive to work at the track, invent new things, and help fix people's problems was still strong as ever.

"My grandfather always had time for everybody," Johnna Crispe says. "He had the right pyramid built up in his life and he seemed to make it all work."

The Bandimere eight grandchildren weren't around to experience their grandfather's earliest exploits in the speed shop, on Pikes Peak, or along the mountainside during the speedway's groundbreaking moments. But they were still able to learn some invaluable lessons about work ethic, perseverance, commitment and faith.

The Value of Hard Work

When Crispe watches her son Cale walk, it reminds her of the distinctive skip that her grandfather had in his step. Bandimere Sr. was always in a hurry and could hardly stand still. In those rare moments when he actually stood in a stationary position, he was always wrestling with something in his pocket–usually some nuts and bolts that would eventually prove useful–and he would repeatedly toss and catch a small tool–usually a screwdriver–with his other hand.

"Grandpa could never stand still and totally focus on the conversation," Crispe adds.

That didn't mean he wasn't listening and it certainly didn't mean that he didn't care. It was simply his way of multitasking and doing his best to make the most of his time. No doubt, that desire to stay alert and ready to move to the next thing was a byproduct of living through The Great Depression and two World Wars. From his time on the farm as a young boy to his days in the speed shop, Bandimere Sr. had spent most of his life cultivating an unmatched work ethic.

Granddaughter Tami Shrader jokes that he loved food and the only way you could slow him down was to plan a meal.

"My grandpa was always working," she says. "But we never felt like we were missing out on anything. It was just the way he was."

Not surprisingly, many of the grandchildren's memories of Bandimere Sr. revolve around his work in the garage or at the track. Crispe remembers one story that has continued to impact she and her older sister long into their adult lives. As pre-teen girls, they routinely spent much of their spare time at the speedway painting, cleaning or whatever chores John Jr. and Lorraine assigned them to complete. On this particular day, they were picking up trash around the concession stand but in reality wasting more time than actually working. Grandpa Bandimere suddenly drove up and hopped out of his car.

"What are you doing," he asked.

"We're picking up trash," they casually replied.

"I need to teach you a lesson about how to pick up trash!" he quickly retorted. "My Frances can do circles around you! Let me show you how to pick up trash!"

At that time, Bandimere Sr. was referring to his second wife who shared his deceased first wife's name. When she picked up trash, she always wore a long skirt or a dress. On the other hand, the granddaughters usually donned much cooler attire such as shorts and halter tops.

"You might want to cover up," Grandpa Bandimere often advised.

At that point, the young girls were no longer amused and showed their frustration with him. And then they got mad.

"We were not going to let Grandpa and Frances have the upper hand," Crispe says. "From that day forward, Tami and I really learned to pour it on and work and sweat and not finish until we were done. We might have been aggravated at him, but we later realized that it was just one of his lessons of love. He loved us and he wanted us to become something."

Although Sporty Bandimere was the youngest of the three siblings, he still spent equal amounts of time working around the track. His list of responsibilities increased throughout his teenage years and Grandpa Bandimere routinely pushed him to the limit.

"We had some bad spots on our asphalt at the track," he explains. "It was our job to bust it up and haul it away so the asphalt company could come in and patch it up and repair it. That was a lot of work. I was out there with no shirt on, a pair of shorts, and some tennis shoes. And my grandpa was next to me in a long sleeve blue work shirt with long pants working next to me. That was his work attire no matter if the temperature was five degrees or 105. He wouldn't take a break for anything. I was sweaty and thirsty and dying out there and he just kept going and going. Of course, if you didn't keep up with him, you heard about it. You had to step up your game or you were in serious trouble. He would work nonstop. And when we finally got a chance to get something to drink, it was well water, which won't hurt you but it doesn't taste very good. He'd take a hose and take a big swig of orange-colored well water. But that's just the way he functioned."

By the time his grandchildren were teenagers, Bandimere Sr. had put in over 20 years into the track. It was his baby and that sentiment often came through loud and clear when anyone damaged or defaced the property. Up until the late 1980s, the facility was mostly covered in gravel. Young drivers would sometimes spin donuts in the parking lot and sling pebbles everywhere. Needless to say, Grandpa Bandimere would find the perpetrators.

"He would storm over there and let them have it," Crispe says. "I don't know what he said to them, but he never cussed. Whatever he said, they were always shaking or crying. And then he would make them rake up every single mark that they had made in the gravel. Of course, after he handed them the rake, he probably followed it up with the Bible."

The Bravest Man Alive

Growing up with Grandpa Bandimere was an adventure. As if spending countless hours at a racetrack built into the side of a mountain wasn't exciting enough, the grandchildren were often treated to a taste of his past life as one of the Denver area's pioneering racers.

Take for instance a typical Sunday drive. Although Bandimere Sr. didn't attend the same church as Bandimere Jr. and his family, he would sometimes visit and that usually resulted in an opportunity for the kids to ride with him to a restaurant for brunch. It was on those Sundays when the family finally got a chance to see him in something other than his blue work shirts and his blue work pants. The most noticeable piece of his Sunday attire was always a colorful tie with a flower print or a Hawaiian-themed design.

"There was a lady from his church that would make him those crazy looking ties," Shrader fondly remembers. "He was a humble man, but he loved those ties. They came into the room long before he did."

Once they were all in Grandpa's car, that's when the real fun began.

"It's a good thing cell phones were not in existence back then," Crispe laughs. "His driving was unbelievable. He drove with one hand while singing or eating. He would talk to whoever was in the passenger seat and look them in the eyes when he was speaking to them. For that moment, he was so engaged in conversation that he almost forgot he was driving. It was like an amusement park every time."

"Go faster! Go faster!" the kids would scream.

When they arrived at their destination, they would get out of the car giggling and laughing. They had just enjoyed the ride of their lives.

Bandimere Sr. took that free spirited, fearless nature to his work at the track. Add to the mix his trademark ingenuity and there was no telling what might happen. After the family bought an old truck with a lift device on the back, Bandimere Sr. looked for a way to extend its reach in order to change light bulbs or work on wiring. The unconventional solution was to strap an aluminum light pole to the truck's extension and mount a basket at the top. With no safety wire or harness, Grandpa Bandimere would climb into the basket and take a 30-foot journey that sometimes went straight up.

Once fully elevated, he and his right hand man Tommy Bricker would go to work.

"They had a great relationship," Sporty Bandimere says. "Grandpa would get in the basket and Tommy would throw him whatever tool he needed. They would throw tools back and forth to each other. It was like they were in a circus. With OSHA (Occupational Safety and Health Administration) and all the workplace regulations today, there's no way they could do those kinds of things now."

Although Bandimere Sr. fell from that basket on more than one occasion, he always managed to shake himself off and climb back in. His ability to bounce back quickly manifested on many occasions and created the perception that he was, at least in Shrader's impressionable mind, "the bravest man alive."

"He would smash his finger and maybe go, 'Ow! Ow! Ow!' but then he'd wrap a dirty rag around it or whatever he could find."

And then there was the day she had been picking up trash at the track and it was time for a lunch break. Grandpa Bandimere sat down nearby and took off his steel toe boot to reveal a blood-soaked sock. A heavy object had fallen on his foot, he revealed, and had nearly taken his toenail completely off.

"It's not a big deal," he calmly stated.

He then got some orange-tinted well water, rinsed out his sock, put the sock back on his foot without a bandage, put the shoe back on and went back to work as if nothing had happened.

In a more extreme example of his high pain tolerance, Bandimere Sr. was helping a neighborhood teenager who couldn't start his car. He pulled one of the spark plugs out and told the boy to give the engine a bump so he could see if there was any compression, but instead he tried to start the car. Grandpa Bandimere's hand was painfully caught between the pulley and the fan.

"He had to tell the kid how to go down to his house down the street, get into his garage, get the tools that he needed and bring them back to him so he could pry the pulley apart and get his hand out," Sporty Bandimere says.

Although the accident nearly severed one of his fingers, Bandimere Sr. showed no signs of discomfort in front of the boy. After the job was done, he quickly covered his injured hand with a rag. Bandimere Sr. later went to the hospital but the youngster never knew the severity of the situation.

Grandpa Bandimere's bravery also showed up in his dealings at the track. Because of his religious convictions, he instituted a rule that no alcohol was allowed in the facility. If he found someone drinking, he would go right behind them and reach over the top and yank a beer from their hands and dump it out on the ground. In some instances, he would take someone's cooler and load it on the back of a truck and drive away.

"I was afraid he was going to get hurt doing that," Shrader says. "You couldn't do that today, but back then it was no big deal to him"

And that wasn't even the most dangerous situation where Bandimere Sr.'s bravery revealed itself. Randy Gager recalls an incident at the track that involved a drunken motorcycle rider, Grandpa Bandimere, his Uncle John, his little brother Russ and his cousin Sporty. At the time, the track didn't have insurance for motorcycle racing, but the intoxicated rider decided to take an unauthorized run during a rain delay. This did not sit well with Grandpa Bandimere.

"As the motorcycle guy finished his run and raced back on the return road, it was obvious he wasn't sticking around," Randy Gager says. "So he headed around the big curved road that led out the facility and sped away. Grandpa flew into action, jumped into his Renault and chased after him. He had no intention of allowing this guy to perpetrate such an offense and get away with it."

John Bandimere Jr. followed suit and took off in *his* Renault with Sporty and Russ, both about eight or nine years old, in the backseat. Randy and his friend Larry took off running across the field. They took an angle in hopes of seeing the action transpire.

"Grandpa motioned and honked for the man to pull over and stop but to no avail," Randy Gager adds. "So Grandpa took matters into his hands and began nudging the bike rider with his car and finally knocked him and his bike off balance and down to the ground."

Now dangerously drunk and angry, the motorcycle driver took off his helmet, swung it and struck Grandpa Bandimere in the head. Just then, Bandimere Jr. came to a screeching halt. He yelled at Sporty and Russ to "stay put!" and rushed to the scene.

"Uncle Johnny threw a tremendous haymaker of a right punch that caught the perpetrator squarely and dropped him like a rock," Randy Gager clearly recalls. "I believe a few more punches found their target before it all ended and the driver was led away by the Sheriff's department. I found out later that Uncle Johnny's knuckles and hand showed signs of the confrontation. But Grandpa, who was the single toughest human being I ever knew, was no worse for the wear."

The Fierce Competitor

Like his brothers and cousins, Rick Gager learned a lot of invaluable lessons from Grandpa Bandimere in a relatively short period of time. Some of his most vivid memories are of a man who was driven to prove that difficult and sometimes seemingly impossible tasks could be accomplished. All he needed was hard work, ingenuity and at times a little bit of that aforementioned bravery that often manifested itself in an inexplicable competitive spirit.

"Maybe that's why he used to drive with his eyes closed," Gager says. "Did somebody tell him he couldn't do it? I don't know, but he did it, and had fun scaring anybody willing to ride with him."

Skip Bandimere grew up with a strong interest in his family's history, particularly the 1950s and his Grandpa's racing exploits at places like Pikes Peak where he famously engineered his 1957 Chevy for driver Gordon Herring to compete in the "Race To The Clouds."

He also has fond memories of spending the day with Grandpa Bandimere at a nostalgic drag racing event where he raced his Cadillac truck. Bandimere Sr. was very enthusiastic to collect and rub off the scratch tickets that Dunkin Donuts was handing out at the event. Hot Rod Magazine later published a picture of Skip and his grandfather from that special day.

"We all lived in his shadow and so much of what we did and thought was a result of what he had done and who he was," he says. "That truck symbolized a wonderful era in my family's life and in automobile history. It's amazing how something like that gets in your blood and drives you on your quest through life."

For Bandimere Sr., competition was often wrapped up in something fun. Rick Gager fondly remembers going to large family lunch gatherings after church at places like Furr's Cafeteria. Grandpa Bandimere especially enjoyed these times together because the meal was traditionally followed by a time of prayer and a Bible study.

Then, it was time for the men to engage in a hearty card game of Rook.

"It was amusing to me to watch these devout men who had moments earlier been engaged in prayer and devotion become so intense and passionate about playing cards," Rick Gager says. "And my grandfather was one of the most intense and competitive."

At Christmas time, Grandpa Bandimere was often the center of a fun game where the rest of the family would challenge him to guess his presents before opening them. The grandkids were amazed as he always figured out what was inside the boxes or gift sacks. The contest grew more spirited over the years as the family would do their best to creatively disguise the gifts by doing things like placing small items in large packages. One year, the guessing game cost David Bandimere a thousand dollars after he lost a friendly bet and failed to fool his crafty father.

Grandpa Bandimere's competitive drive naturally spilled over to the track where during the summer, he and his grandkids would gather for some exhilarating fun with fireworks. One day, he brought a tin can, a large iron tube and some M-80s. The first M-80 shot the can out of the tube into the air with a resounding "Boom!" But that wasn't good enough for Bandimere Sr.

"He tried two M-80s, and then three, and finally put enough inside the tube to send that can so far in the air that it was several seconds before it came back into sight," Rick Gager recalls. "We watched with amazement, from behind cover of course, wondering if that can ever return to earth."

Bandimere Jr. continues to harbor his father's love for fireworks today at the racetrack through the orchestration of fireworks displays at events during the racing season.

And then there was his legendary race car affectionately known as "Grandpa's Toy." Bandimere Sr. loved Renault cars. His favorite was a Chevy powered white Renault 16 that he had supercharged with the famed "black box" that is still in grandson Sporty Bandimere's '55 Chevy today.

Even into his late 70s, Bandimere Sr. would drive that car down the quarter-mile track on several occasions. But for Rick Gager, the most memorable pass took place when neighbor, fellow racer and family friend Frank Peterson asked Grandpa Bandimere to take Peterson's car for a test run. Peterson had been testing and tuning the car all night but wasn't getting the results he wanted.

"I remember watching my grandfather sit in that car at the starting line as he waited for the Christmas tree lights to count down," Rick Gager says. "Suddenly, the car was streaking down the track as Grandpa had pulled of the perfect hole shot and taken the car for its best run of the night."

The Repurposed Driven Life

Bandimere Sr. was notoriously tight with his money. Like many Depression-era survivors, he placed great value on sweat equity and making the most out of what was already in his hand.

"Everything had to be bought at a swap meet or an auction or a flea market," Sporty Bandimere says. "A lot of times he would take old equipment that he had in the basement and he would fix it up and make it work for whatever the need was at the time."

Even though Bandimere Sr. had already turned the track over to his son John Bandimere Jr., the tug-of-war between dueling approaches to business still remained.

"When my dad when out and spent money on the grandstands and the timing system, that was pretty difficult for my grandpa to deal with," Sporty Bandimere adds. "Grandpa never took loans out or spent a lot of money, so that made it challenging for my dad. He knew that things needed to be done to bring people in. We needed to add amenities to make things better around the track."

That didn't stop Grandpa Bandimere from trying his hardest to make contributions the old fashioned way. As much as she might try, Shrader can't shake the lingering memories of his infamous attempt at building the track's first port-a-johns.

"We called them the tin cans," she says. "They were made out of metal and Grandpa would pour concrete floors and then dig a hole and put in a 12-inch clay pipe. He would put a phone book inside and that's what you would use for toilet paper. They were just awful."

But Bandimere Sr. was rather proud of his efforts mostly because he had repurposed so much material. Shrader now understands that he was simply being a good steward of the things that God had given him. She also saw, however, a fighting spirit within the context of that can do attitude. It "fueled his fire" when someone told Grandpa Bandimere he couldn't do something.

Sporty Bandimere, who caught the racing bug at a young age, was always impressed with his grandfather's incredible mechanical mind and his ability to take what he already had and make it even better.

"Grandpa invented so many different things," he says. "If he had an idea, next thing you knew he was making it. He wanted to find ways to do jobs better and be more efficient. He understood the automobile extremely well. He knew how to make it work whether it was putting a supercharger on a small block Chevy or building rocker arm clips to keep oil from splashing while adjusting the valves. And he never stopped thinking of new things to develop. He'd be in the middle of doing something and all of the sudden he'd quit and go over and start working on some other idea."

Despite all of his quirks about money and his rigid views on stewardship, Grandpa Bandimere's grandchildren could always count on him for the things that truly mattered most.

"He might buy your lunch every once in a while, but if you were crushed and needed a shoulder to cry on or if you needed some really good advice, you could also count on getting his insight," Crispe says. "That was the best payment ever."

The Steadfast Faith

As they each got old enough to drive, the grandchildren took turns racing Grandpa's Toy at the high school drags. By the time Johnna Crispe got her opportunity to get behind the wheel, her older sister and younger brother had already taken the iconic car for a ride down the track.

"I lost sleep over it," she says. "I was so excited. I was thinking about how good I would look in that car."

But the day she was scheduled to race, bad weather swept through Morrison and forced the event to move from Saturday to the following day. This created a problem for Bandimere Sr. and a frustrating situation for Crispe.

"Honey," he said. *"You know I can't let that car race on a Sunday."*

Crispe was furious. *He* wasn't the one who was going to be out there racing. Why did Grandpa Bandimere's convictions have to carry over to her?

"As the years have gone by, I've come to realize that it was a lesson of love," she says. "He loved the Lord and racing on Sunday was something he said he wouldn't do. I forgave him for that, but it was a really hard lesson."

"He was a man of great spiritual fervor and conviction," Skip Bandimere adds. "I know that there were many points in his life where he had to stand on what he believed was clearly from God."

But Bandimere Sr. never forced his viewpoint or his Christian beliefs down people's throats. Rather, his actions spoke louder than words.

"You knew where my Grandpa Bandimere stood when it came to his faith," Shrader says. "You didn't even need to ask him. You just knew. If I had a boyfriend, I didn't have to ask if Grandpa was going to like him. I just knew by the way he acted around that person. He never wavered. And he wasn't mean about it. You just knew where he was coming from. Who you saw was who he was."

His grandchildren knew he wasn't perfect. They knew that he struggled sometimes as a husband, father, grandfather and businessman. But as Rick Gager conveys, they also knew that he loved God and wasn't ashamed to be a Christian.

"Many think his greatest legacy is leaving the business to his family," he says. "The truth is his greatest legacy was his life of faith. His desire was to use his love for cars and racing to share faith with as many as possible. I have always respected his love and devotion to Jesus."

As is often typical with young people, the grandchildren didn't always appreciate their grandfather's relentless work ethic, his fearless nature, his frustrating frugality, or his unwavering spiritual convictions. But over time, their admiration has exponentially grown.

"It's so much easier now to understand how hard of a worker my grandpa was," Sporty Bandimere says. "I always knew how intelligent he was when it came to automotive and mechanical things. I always knew that he was a Christian and that he loved the Lord. I would hear him witness to people. I would see him hand out Bibles to people. I knew he had morals and values and integrity. There were certain things he did and certain things he didn't do. Without dwelling on it as a kid, I knew those things about my grandfather, and those experiences have had a profound and lasting impact."

13
Glory Days

By the late 1970s, John Bandimere Jr. had taken a more active role in track management. He began bringing larger and more frequent races into Morrison to help financially support the business. That led to a conversation with NHRA West Central director Darrell Zimmerman about bringing a national event to Colorado.

"As someone who grew up in the area, I always thought we should have a national event in Denver," Zimmerman says. "So consequently, the Bandimere family kept working on the facility to the point where I felt it could handle it. That's when I proposed it to the NHRA Board of Directors. They flew to Denver to look at the speedway and agreed to put a national event there."

Prior to 1978, Bandimere Speedway had hosted regional events and points races. But the arrival of the Mile-High NHRA Sportsnationals represented a significant competitive jump.

"One of the things that was attractive about Denver was the market," former NHRA President Dallas Gardner says. "We were growing at that point and to be able to compete in the motorsports world at that level, we needed to be in the top markets. We needed to cover markets that the other organizations weren't in. Denver provided a very pristine market for us."

The Mile-High NHRA Sportsnationals was a one-time event that ran in 1978. Serving as a test run for a national event, it didn't run the Top Fuel, Funny Car or Pro Stock divisions, but rather featured Top Alcohol Dragsters, Top Alcohol Funny Cars and sportsman classes such as Competition Eliminator, Stock and Super Stock.

"We knew the Bandimere family was committed to the sport," Gardner says. "They were committed to NHRA. John Sr. was the pioneer of the sport in that part of the country. There was a lot of credibility that came with the Bandimere name."

Star Struck

July of 1979 was a historic time at Bandimere Speedway and welcomed the first Mile-High NHRA Nationals. The track had sufficiently proven the year before that it could handle a large-scale event.

But that date has also been the source of a recurring nightmare for David Bandimere and his wife Barbara.

One of their many roles at the speedway was to sell tickets to the spectators as they arrived at any given event. Previous to 1979, fans drove in front of the office building and bought tickets through the window of their car before parking and walking into the main gate. Nothing could prepare them for what was about to happen.

"We were working the gates together and we had hired some help," David Bandimere explains. "The people had parked en masse everywhere–in places we didn't anticipate that they would park. When those lower gates got opened, we saw a mass of humanity coming at us. We only had two selling booths with four lanes and all were full of cars. There was more foot traffic than we could handle coming up the drive entrance. I still wake up in the middle of the night sometimes seeing that horde of people coming up from that gate."

Those who walked up to buy tickets were caught standing in a ferocious wind. David Bandimere and his crew were trying to handle money, but inevitably some paper currency blew out of their hands. As had become customary at previous events, Bandimere Sr. would walk the fence line afterwards and see how much cash he could find.

To help rectify the problem, David Bandimere retrieved his Chevy Astro van as quickly as he could. He had two people get into the side of the van in an effort to create an additional walk-up lane. Rope was used to try and separate the cars from the pedestrian traffic.

"I don't know how much money we lost that day," he says. "We couldn't control it. It was an unbelievable moment. Who knows how many walked in with no regard for our plight or without paying?"

"You never told me that," Bandimere Jr. responds upon hearing that story for the first time some 35 years later.

"We didn't want to give you nightmares like ours," Barbara Bandimere replies amid a roar of laughter.

With this unexpected trouble also came an entourage of NHRA employees that took over much of the responsibility that the local crew was accustomed to handling. George Abbas was the track PA announcer but gave way to legendary NHRA voice Dave McClelland. Even his duties in the tower became obsolete as NHRA officials managed the timing system not to mention tech inspection and the starting line.

"It was exciting," Abbas says. "All of the top names from drag racing were there."

Bandimere Jr.'s daughter Tami Shrader remembers seeing famous drag racing personalities like NHRA Founder Wally Parks and big time racers like Kenny Bernstein and Don Garlits.

"I was a little star struck by all of that," she admits.

Shrader still enjoys teasing her older sister Johnna Crispe over her infatuation with Don "The Snake" Prudomme. Crispe, a teenager at the time, knew everything about the four-time funny car champion including his birthdate, his statistics and his family, and was in heaven when she had her picture taken with him at an NHRA race in Pomona, California.

"She was in love with Don Prudhomme," Shrader laughs with eyes rolled upward. "But when he came to our track, he didn't remember who she was and was more involved with racing instead of this infatuated young fan. So she got over that real fast."

Although former NHRA announcer Dave McClelland had already met Bandimere Jr. at national track operators meetings and related functions, his first experience at the speedway didn't take place until that first Mile-High NHRA Nationals. His first impression has yet to fade.

"I was blown away primarily because of the location," McClelland says. "My admiration went out to John Sr. who had the idea of using the mountainside and providing a flat surface for a drag strip. You've got two great advantages. You've got unrestricted sight lines from wherever you sit in the grandstands. And secondly, if the fan gets bored with the racing, he or she can just look across the valley and enjoy the scenery. There are all kinds of attractions from the spectator's point of view."

At that first national event, Kelly Brown won the Top Fuel division, Billy Meyer took home the Funny Car title and Randy Humphrey claimed Pro Stock honors. But for the Bandimere family, the inaugural Mile-High NHRA Nationals had instantly elevated the track and placed Morrison, Colorado, on the drag racing world's map.

Moving Parts

While Bandimere Speedway was gaining notoriety thanks in great part to the early success of the Mile-High NHRA Nationals, the family auto parts business was still going strong. By the early 1980s, there were four stores, a warehouse and a machine shop.

In hindsight, however, David Bandimere believes that the family grew the business too fast and it could no longer sustain itself. He particularly feels responsible for attempting to move the stores into automation, something that is commonplace today and allows for employees to work in a parts store without actually knowing much about cars.

"Everything is done for them," David Bandimere explains. "Everything is on a screen. That kind of automated technology was just starting in the 1980s, but it wasn't the right time for our stores. I forced it too soon and it cost us an arm and a leg."

In 1983, Bandimere Jr. found an outside company that was willing to buy the stores. That freed the family up to pursue other ventures that would benefit the track with embroidery services and special apparel. Johnna Crispe was part of this venture and now manages Bandimere Speedway's souvenir and merchandising portion of the business.

As the Bandimere family opted out of the parts business, it helped to ease the tensions between them and the Kenz & Leslie group.

"Before then, John Jr., David and I were, for a lack of a better term, at each other's throats," Ron Leslie says. "I was working in a warehouse trying to sell parts. John Jr. and David were trying to do the retail thing and also selling parts through their warehouse. But there was a point where the Bandimere's were buying pieces from us to keep their stores going. That competitive edge kind of trimmed off when they closed down that portion of their operation."

From there, the focus turned towards Bandimere Speedway where John Jr. handled the programming. David worked with the public and dealt with souvenirs, concessions, fuel and auto parts sales, while his wife Barbara took care of the finances and ticketing. Regardless of these assignments, everyone pitched in where needed.

And although the parts stores were now in the family's past, they continue to provide countless positive memories.

"The stores were a blessing," David Bandimere says. "Our folks started that business and it answered a lot of needs for many years. We were blessed with a lot of amazing people that worked for us in those stores. Many of these people ended up coming out to the speedway and helping us because of some very personal connections that were made over the years."

Big Shoes

In 1979, John Bandimere Sr. was inducted into the Colorado Motorsports Hall of Fame. It was an appropriate honor for the man who had so greatly impacted the car performance community throughout Denver and pioneered the city's vibrant drag racing scene.

It was an odd time for Bandimere Sr. He was slowly stepping away from day-to-day operations at the racetrack while remaining observant of its steady growth although it wasn't exactly the way he had imagined it.

"He was pleased with how well the business was doing," Lorraine Bandimere says. "He just didn't want to spend any money to make it a greater success. That was the division between him and his sons."

According to David Bandimere, his aversion to financial investment was a product of his generation.

"The Depression had a huge impact on the people that went through it," he says. "Dad didn't understand very well the value of time. But he valued whatever he had in his hands that he could work with."

Still, as he became less physically able to help out, Bandimere Sr. wanted to be around the action.

"I think dad really appreciated what was happening out here," Joanna Gager says. "He loved to watch John Jr. race. I used to take him with me to the track and he would just beam when Johnny raced."

In April of 1985, Bandimere Sr.'s second wife Frances passed away. By summer time, he no longer had the strength to do routine, simple tasks such as fixing the taillight on a car. But one thing he never lost was his sense of humor.

"I remember going to a restaurant one Sunday night after church with the whole family," grandson-in-law Larry Crispe says. "As we were sitting at the table, he was drinking coffee. With every sip or unconscious movement, he kept inching it further and further towards the edge of the table. I looked over at my wife Johnna nervously thinking he was about to drop that cup and spill it everywhere. At that moment, he slid it just enough to the edge to the point where we were all feeling very uneasy. With a sly but slow movement, he pretended that he was dropping the cup and then looked up at us with a big grin on his face.

"You all thought I was going to spill my coffee didn't you? Bandimere Sr. coyly asked. "Did I scare you?"

Crispe will never forget learning yet another lesson about Grandpa Bandimere's witty personality and clever mind. While the family was zeroing in on his failing missteps, he was actually planning the joke on them all along.

In 1986, Bandimere Sr. moved in with David's family and had his bedroom next to his granddaughter Susan. Now married with the last name Brown, she was 14 years old at the time and had never seen her grandfather as anything but strong. As she watched her parents and her aunt Joanna care for him, she experienced both heartwarming and confusing emotions.

One April evening, Susan lay upstairs in the hall and listened to her grandfather tell her parents about all of his plans and ideas for the future.

"He told them that he would probably outlive us all and that he would be at my wedding," she affectionately remembers. "He was feeling strong again and full of life, so the next morning I went to school and didn't check on him like I always had done before."

A few hours later, she was called into the office and informed that Grandpa Bandimere had passed away. Devastated by the news, Susan sat in the hall and cried.

"When I went in to check on Dad that morning, I could not believe it," David Bandimere says. "I must have gone in and out of the room a dozen times to be sure if he was gone. I was by Mom's bedside when she passed away and I thought and prayed over the years as to how to prepare for Dad's passing. The Lord has helped me understand that all things, even family and relationships are on loan. The victory is in living thankfully for each gift while we have it and recognize these are gifts for a time, not possessions. It has made a big difference in my life when it comes time to let go."

At Riverside Baptist Church, David's daughter Susan was one of over 1,000 people that had gathered to pay tribute to Bandimere Sr. Although she missed him dearly, she was also grateful for the legacy that he and her grandmother Frances had left behind. Bandimere Sr. didn't make it to her wedding after all, but he had shown her what true love looked like.

Family friend and former Denver Area Youth for Christ director Jim Groen attended Bandimere Sr.'s funeral and was one of the officiates. Groen was emotionally moved as Bandimere Jr. and David Bandimere spoke about their father.

"He was very popular in Denver," Groen says. "You could see that he was very loved throughout the city."

David Beckman reminisced about the memorial service just six weeks before he passed away in March of 2014.

"There was a huge crowd there," he said. "I was scared to death. I regarded it one of the great, great privileges in my life–to preach at John's funeral."

Ironically, or perhaps providentially, Beckman stood before the gatherers as someone whose life had been eternally changed because of his relationship with the man that they were there to honor.

"We've always wanted to make sure that people understand that the track was started by a man and a woman who loved the Lord and who loved kids," Bandimere Jr. says. "David Beckman was one of those kids. The testament of their love for him is that he loved them back."

For Bob Janowski, the funeral took him back in time to a friendship that revolved around their shared hunger for knowledge about horsepower and superchargers and their desire to put that knowledge to work. But the real bond was as brothers in Christ.

"Jesus died for our sins, rose again, and ascended into Heaven," Janowski says. "That means that John Sr. and I not only shared wonderful times and wonderful camaraderie here on earth, but that we will see each other again and our friendship will be blessed by God for eternity."

Sporty Bandimere was 20 years old when Bandimere Sr. passed away. With that loss came a powerful revelation. Until then, he had always thought of his Grandpa as the high performance guy who owned an auto parts store and built a racetrack.

"That's who he was and who the family was," he adds.

But over the following weeks and months, he would strike up conversations with people who knew his grandfather well and they usually talked about other characteristics that made him special.

"Your grandfather impressed me because he wouldn't do certain things," some would say.

"You know, your grandpa was the first one who talked to me about Jesus," others would share. "He was the one who led me to the Lord."

As these sobering nuggets of reality were dropped into Sporty Bandimere's spirit, he began to realize that it wasn't about the cars. It wasn't even about the racetrack or performance. It was about Christ and the Kingdom. He simply used those things as tools to communicate with others.

Not long after the funeral, he attended a team building seminar where each person was required to speak to the others and convince them about a certain point they were trying to make. Each member of the audience would stand up once they were persuaded to do so. The speaker wasn't allowed to stop talking until everyone was standing.

Sporty Bandimere had all night to come up with a topic for the next morning's exercise. When it was his turn to speak, he had no idea what he was going to say. Instead, he burst into tears. Everyone stood up before he said a single word.

As he regained his composure, he finally said these words:

"I feel like I have such big shoes to fill that my grandfather has left and that my father will be leaving someday," he passionately conveyed. "I don't know if I can ever fill those."

In that moment, Sporty Bandimere was feeling the weight of his grandfather's legacy of humility and compassion for others.

"He didn't have a lot of money," he says. "He didn't have a lot of things. But he loved the Lord and he wasn't afraid to share that with others. At the end of the day, that's what people remember about him–his demeanor, his personal touch and his willingness to share scripture and the Lord. He was a man that lived his life the way it should be lived. He knew what truly mattered."

14
Mountain Moving

Bandimere Speedway had only been hosting the Mile-High NHRA Nationals for a few years before rumblings of the track's inadequate facilities could be heard behind the scenes. Not coincidentally, concerns initially surfaced around 1984 when Dallas Gardner was elevated from his position as NHRA executive vice president and general manager to replace Wally Parks as the organization's president.

Gardner equated the NHRA's affiliate race tracks to the stadiums and arenas of other professional sports and emphasized the importance of those facilities to fan marketability.

"We need to improve our ballparks," he has often said.

In 1986, the Texas Motorplex opened up about 40 miles south of Dallas in Ennis. It was the first NHRA track to be labeled a "super track," and was ironically built by Billy Meyer, the funny car driver who won the inaugural Mile-High NHRA Nationals back in 1979. Gardner was pushing for existing tracks to rise to that level of sophistication.

Conversation between Gardner and the Bandimere Jr. had been ongoing but nothing as serious as the meeting that took place in the Bandimere Speedway conference room immediately following the 1987 Mile-High NHRA Nationals. Gardner sat across the table from Bandimere Jr. to deliver an ultimatum.

Bandimere Jr. knew what was coming. His mind flashed back to an incident that had taken place a few days earlier. During the high profile NHRA event, the worker that had been hired to pump the port-a-johns got drunk and was unable to do his job. Bandimere Jr. jumped into action and hotwired the pumping truck and took care of the problem on his own. Gardner saw the episode unfold before his eyes. And while he didn't bring up that particular moment, he did lay out a long list of concerns.

"I told them we couldn't bring the national event back unless they committed to do certain things with the facility," Gardner says. "The racetrack was good. We didn't have any safety issues. But for the spectators' sake and for it to become a major national event, things were going to have to change."

One of the biggest issues was fan visibility. At the other race-tracks, fans could go into the pits and watch the teams work on the cars. It's one of the aspects of NHRA that makes it unique from others motorsports. But at Bandimere Speedway, the fans were sitting on one side of the track and the pits were on the other side. This made it difficult for the spectators to get to the race cars.

"That was a hard conversation to have," Gardner adds. "We really liked the family and we wanted to continue doing business with them. In talking to John Jr., I wasn't sure if the family would be willing to make those changes. It really required a total commitment. I know John got a lot of feedback from the family and spent a lot of nights wrestling with himself on that decision."

Before the meeting concluded, Bandimere Jr. posed an important question.

"If we make the necessary improvements, do I have your assurance that this event will come back to Bandimere Speedway?" he asked.

"Yes," Gardner simply replied.

That led to a series of requests from Bandimere Jr..

First, he wanted a sabbatical. The track would need to take the next year off in order to have time to renovate and update the facilities.

Secondly, he wanted NHRA to send in a group of people to provide a list of things that needed to be done and a plan of action to get the job done.

Finally, Bandimere Jr. asked for a commitment from Gardner to work on securing a title sponsor for the Mile-High NHRA Nationals.

Gardner agreed to all three items on the list.

After a time of prayerful consideration, the family met in the speedway conference room to discuss their options. Bandimere Jr. still has the notes that were written on an easel pad for everyone to clearly see as they brainstormed a plan of action:

1. Stay like we are. Don't worry about stepping up.

The family didn't have to do what the NHRA wanted. They didn't have to host a national event. They could continue hosting smaller events and serving the local and regional racers.

2. Get out all together.

3. Spend $$ and stay for ___ years.

The family discussed the possibility of making the investment and commitment to stay in that location for at least another 10 years. Little did they know that the 10-year commitment would be much longer.

4. Start our own brand new facility.

5. Partner with another group to start another racetrack.

In that meeting room, the Bandimere family unanimously voted for the third option. They all supported the decision to move forward and make the improvements necessary to keep the NHRA national event.

"It just boiled down to staying where they were," former NHRA Division Five Director Darrell Zimmerman says. "It was a very good location and there was only one setting in the world like the side of that mountain. There was never going to be another track built that way anywhere."

Even after that meeting, there was still much uncertainty about how to make it all work. It certainly helped that the option of borrowing money was now on the table. Previously, Bandimere Sr. had instituted an unwritten rule against the practice. The family was also going to need help from the NHRA to get advice on specific details of the renovation. Thankfully, Gardner stood by his promise and offered Zimmerman, Wayne McMurtry, Carl Olson, and some other experts to help navigate the process.

But at the end of the day, it was going to take a lot of hard work and reliance on the people that had brought the track to this point. It also meant reaching out to Larry Crispe who had worked at Bandimere Speedway as a teenager and young adult. Bandimere Jr. called his son-in-law who at the time was working for the University of Denver in its research and development department. When they met in Bandimere Jr.'s office, Crispe agreed to take the job as director of operations, but under one condition.

"I'll come back," he said. "But I don't want to pick up trash."

Bandimere Jr. says it was one of the best decisions he ever made. Crispe emerged to serve as the glue that kept the project moving in the right direction.

Over the next year and a half, the Bandimere family worked tirelessly to keep the dream alive. Sporty Bandimere was still a college student at the time and didn't yet have many responsibilities at the track. But he remembers being in that conference room when the decision was made.

"I never doubted it," he says. "We knew that we were going to move forward. We were going to trust that God would get us to where He wanted us to be."

Speedway or the Highway

A few years before the family made the decision to renovate the facility, there was another complicated issue that had threatened the speedway's very existence. It revolved around the development of Highway C-470. Originally referred to as I-470, the highway was first proposed in 1973 but political infighting and resistance from some anti-tax groups led to nearly 10 years of delay.

As construction grew closer, the Colorado Department of Transportation (CDOT) had to decide on three possible locations for the W-470 portion of the highway.

The most desirable location was to run it right along the hogback. This, of course, would have taken the highway right through the racetrack and forced its closure. Another option was to push the highway much further east from the track. A third option was to run the highway just slightly east of the track.

As CDOT made a play for its first choice, problems arose when officials realized that their plans would put the highway in the path of the Rooney Ranch Homestead, which sat just to the north of Bandimere Speedway. This historical site remains one of the oldest ranches in Jefferson County and is thought to be one of the earliest Indian Trading posts in the region. There was no way CDOT would get permission to take this route. The timely revelation literally saved Bandimere Speedway from being put out of business.

So instead, highway officials decided to run the W-470 portion just to the east of the track and then along the hogback where possible. The plan still required some of the Bandimere property. CDOT, therefore, claimed imminent domain and took the land it needed for the transit development. By law, the officials had to make offers to each landowner that was affected. CDOT's offer to the Bandimere family was well below the land's true value so they prepared a condemnation case that would allow them to request a certain amount of money in return.

A one-year battle ensued and led to a court date where the judge would decide the family's case against CDOT. But two weeks before the hearing, the highway officials reached out with an offer that the Bandimere's would accept. Strangely, the money wasn't what closed the deal.

There was a five-acre piece of land on the north end of the speedway that CDOT had condemned and confiscated from another landowner. Bandimere Jr. agreed to accept their offer if the family could also have the adjacent property. CDOT wasn't excited to give away the land that they had just paid for, but took the deal nonetheless.

The speedway lost its front entrances due to the highway encroachment, but that turned out to be a positive result. The family had always struggled with poor access to the track. Fans and racers could only get there from Rooney Road via West Alameda Avenue or Morrison Road. It was difficult to get people in and out of the facility. Once the highway was completed, it would give greater access to future patrons.

And ironically, the highway department actually built two new entrances to the track. Those entrances, now simply referred to as Gates A and B, provide easier transit in and out of the facility than ever before.

Once the family knew where the highway was going to go, they were able to move forward with their renovation plans.

Retired NHRA official Wayne McMurtry says strong relationships saved the track from completely going dark.

"John Jr. had a relationship with his racers that allowed him to have open trenches with planks over them so the drivers could still come in and test and run a few small races," McMurtry says. "The racers never complained. And he still has that relationship with them today. He's a patriarch of NHRA track operators. His ability to get it done and work with the neighbors was a big reason it worked."

Solid Rock

For race fans that haven't attended Bandimere Speedway prior to the 1989 season, it might be hard to envision the massive changes that took place with both the addition of manmade structures and the large amounts of earth that was literally removed to create more space.

With the construction of Highway C-470, the Bandimere property lost a significant amount of property, but in exchange gained greater access. Previously, the entire east side of the property was concealed by a high berm. Before Bandimere Sr. purchased the land, the valley behind that natural dirt barrier served as a natural breeding ground for cattle and horses. Removing the berm allowed the speedway to be seen from C-470 and exposed it to the approximate 90,000 cars that drive by each day.

Still, the speedway needed more land to accommodate NHRA's desire for a more fan-friendly race day experience. Dallas Gardner wanted the Bandimere family to make the pits more accessible to the spectators that enjoyed mingling with the drivers and watching the crews work on the cars between sessions. This meant exploring the possibility of pushing the mountain back.

But first, the family had to determine if the structure could even handle such movement. Jefferson County officials weren't going to allow them to cut into the hogback unless it could be proven that there would be no erosion and that the mountain would not fall down. To that end, the family hired two geologists in the hopes of garnering their expert opinions.

There was no guarantee that they would be able to cut into the mountain so severely without creating shifts or slides. One particular concern was the presence of a fault line in the valley east of the mountain known as the Golden Fault.

Amazingly, both geologists came back with a good report. The mountain was completely stable. There was no evidence that moving dirt would cause the mountain to slide. The plan to cut into the hogback could move forward.

Bandimere Jr. purchased an ambient dust permit for $15 and hired a company to begin moving the dirt. As heavy construction on the C-470 was taking place simultaneously just a few hundred yards away, no one seemed to notice that earthmoving vehicles were driving into Bandimere Speedway and starting to move the mountainside.

The process wasn't easy. The rock had to be busted out with dynamite. And then D9 Cats wielding rippers with huge steel teeth were dropped into the mountain and pulled back, bringing large pieces down at once. The teeth cuts are still visible today.

The earth that was removed was relocated to the far north end of the track to help fill the five-acre hole that the Bandimere family had acquired in its deal with CDOT. What was once a worthless piece of land was now being prepared to serve as an overflow pit area.

When C-470 was completed in late 1988, there was a bridge dedication over Morrison Road in plain sight of Bandimere Speedway where dirt was still being moved. County officials finally became aware of what was going on and red tagged the construction efforts. But the shutdown only lasted for 24 hours thanks to the permit that Bandimere Jr. had legally obtained.

The family estimates that four million yards of dirt have been moved since the track started in 1958. Much of that took place during the massive renovation project 30 years later. It was truly a miracle that the mountain was able to sustain such severe cuts. Ever since then, the structure has remained solid as a rock. The Bandimere family has no doubt that God's hand has kept the mountain steady and secure.

Shaky Ground

While there was good news involving the difficult task of moving back the mountain, plenty of other challenges stood in the Bandimere family's way. One of the chief issues was the enormous amount of money that needed to be secured in order to move forward.

The Bandimere's took the money they had received from the highway department along with some of their own money and put out construction bids for the various renovation projects. Part of their decision to spend those compensated funds was to avoid heavy taxation. Investing the money back into the facility made it tax-free.

But problems arose with the estimate of how much dirt would need to be moved. Paying a rate of one dollar per yard, there were 800,000 more yards of dirt to move than was anticipated. This put the project $800,000 over budget.

Bandimere Jr. had already been working on funding when the need for even more money arose. He had not applied for a construction loan but instead had thought they could use the cash in hand to get things started. Once things finished, Bandimere Jr. anticipated that the permanent loan he had acquired would kick in and he would be able to pay the contractors.

This worked well for a while. Over what would ultimately be about a six-month period, contractors would take a draw from the Bandimere money to pay their workers. But then disaster struck. As the funds began to dissipate, Bandimere Jr. called the prominent Texas-based Savings & Loan that held the speedway's permanent loan. He was going to request a draw off the loan to pay the contractors. Instead, he was informed that the S&L had gone bankrupt.

As the cash flow dried up, workers started to walk off the job. For three days, in fact, construction came to a complete halt. Bandimere Jr. couldn't afford to lose any time. He met with a friend from high school who had gone on to become a very successful businessman. After lecturing Bandimere Jr. about taking on the project in the first place, he then took him to a banker downtown and told him to help John with his needs.

Bandimere Jr. requested $500,000. His friend co-signed for the loan. But first, he made Bandimere Jr. sign a paper that gave him ownership of the speedway if the loan could not be repaid.

That money was enough to keep everyone on the job. It didn't take long for everyone to get caught back up in the sense of urgency.

The Bandimere family had yet another opportunity to rely on their faith about 18 months before the track's reopening. Larry Crispe, Bandimere Jr.'s son-in-law and director of operations, was

standing on the steel bleachers on the east side of the track one afternoon when they began to tremble under his feet. He alertly headed
for his vehicle and drove away.

Moments later, a powerful windstorm whipped through the valley and lifted the bleachers off the ground. By the time the gusts had
subsided, the bleachers had been twisted together like a pretzel and
landed partially on the racing surface. Had Crispe not left the
premises, he would have likely been crushed or possibly even killed.

The bleachers were insured. When the adjustor came to assess
the claim, Bandimere Jr. asked what the insurance company was
going to do with the mangled remains.

"Pay someone to remove them for scrap metal," he said.

"Would you allow us to scrap them?" Bandimere Jr. asked.

*"Sure," the adjustor replied. "Saves us money, so you can have them if
you want them."*

This was another answer to prayer. Over the next several weeks,
family, friends and even many of the local racers came out to the
track and helped take the bleachers apart, straighten the pieces and
then finally reassemble them into their original form. Popping the
bolts from the disfigured pieces was at times a risky proposition. But
the hard work paid off. Those bleachers are still used today.

It was in 1988, about midway through the renovation, when Joe
Hilger first arrived at Bandimere Speedway to check on the family's
progress. Hilger was the Mopar Parts Marketing Director and his
employer had just begun talks with NHRA about the title rights for
the Mile-High Nationals.

A year later, in March of 1989, Hilger came back to the track
with his wife and son en route to a skiing trip. Not long before that
visit, he had enthusiastically talked to his superiors about the big
event coming up in July. Mopar Parts had agreed to sponsor the
event.

Much to his surprise, much to his surprise, construction was still
going on and didn't seem close to finishing in time for the scheduled
event. Hilger also noticed the eastside bleachers that were still being
cut apart, straightened and repaired. Although he had his doubts,
Bandimere Jr. did his best to reassure him otherwise.

"It's taken care of," Bandimere Jr. said. "This will happen."

As Hilger and his family left the facility, his wife turned to him with a serious question.

"Joe, tell me again when this event is going to happen?" she asked.

"July," he responded.

"Will you have a job is they don't get it done? she then inquired.

"I don't know."

Somehow, Hilger had a sense of calm as he drove away. Even though he knew it would take a miracle for the Bandimere family to pull off the enormous feat, he trusted that they knew what they were doing.

"They are outstanding individuals and well grounded," Hilger says. "They have their moral compass set right and they're going in the right direction. They have vision and they know where they are headed."

In was two months later, on May 10, 1989 when ground was finally broken on the new control tower, just two months before the scheduled debut of the newly sponsored Mopar Parts Mile-High NHRA Nationals. Pennzoil executive and family friend Doug Miller was in Houston at the time, but kept close tabs on what was going on in Denver.

"John Jr. made all of his track sponsors aware of his progress," Miller says. "He told us what was going on. Even though I was living in Houston, my roots and my extended family were still in Colorado. So I made regular trips back."

Miller was confident in Bandimere Jr. as a man of his word, but behind the scenes there were land speculators lined up to get a piece of the valuable real estate should something go awry.

"Even though Colorado isn't the largest populated state in the U.S., it was one of the highest market share areas for Pennzoil," Miller says. "We did have discussions about what would happen if the track went away. We didn't know how we would replace the marketing exposure that we had."

It wasn't just NHRA and the sponsors that were concerned. Racers like Ron Neff watched from a distance and waited patiently as the track's reopening drew closer.

"The thing that really bothered a lot of racers for a long time was that the races used to be on Saturday night," Neff says. "With the races on Saturday night in the middle of July, the temperature was so much nicer. Now we were going to be moving the finals to Sunday and the hotter conditions. But we were mostly afraid that some of the improvements NHRA was requesting might put the Bandimere family in financial dire straits. We were all rooting for them to get the job done."

15

Rebirth of a Dream

On July 18, 1989, the gates were open for the Mopar Parts Mile-High NHRA Nationals. Just 30 minutes earlier, crewmembers had just finished laying down asphalt and the last patch of sod around the brand new tower that overlooked the starting line. Electricians were likewise completing the last bit of wiring. Even the staging lanes were still being paved a day earlier during registration and tech inspection.

The renovation was supposed to cost $3.7 million but instead was completed with a $4.2 million price tag. One of the most noticeable differences was the seating capacity that increased from about 8,000 to over 27,500. The pit areas had been moved to the widened area that sat between the hogback mountain and expanded grandstands on the west side of the track.

Seemingly overnight, the Bandimere family had earned a higher measure of respect from the community. This day, in essence, represented the rebirth of a dream that had first been placed in John Bandimere Sr.'s heart back in that old speed shop on Benton Street.

Bruce Tawson was one of many who were amazed that the Bandimere family had successfully completed the transformation. Because of his previous work at Continental Divide Raceway, he understood better than most just how difficult the process had been.

"It was unbelievable," Tawson says. "Most people thought there was no way they could do it. It was a gutsy move and it took a lot of trust and confidence on their part. Everyone was grateful because the national event was a big deal throughout the Rocky Mountains. To actually see it happen was awesome. It was just unbelievable."

Former NHRA official Wayne McMurtry had no doubt that the track would reopen on time, but fully understands why others might not have felt the same.

"I had several years of experience watching other projects," he says. "If someone is looking at it from an untrained eye, they might have thought there was no way it would ever happen. It went down to the wire, but we were ready to accept less than perfect in order to keep the event going."

NHRA Pro Stock championship racer Mike Edwards agrees. He knew the Bandimere family well enough to have total faith in their ability (and their trust in God) to pull through for the city of Denver and the entire drag racing community.

"I always thought it would come back," Edwards says. "I knew how committed they were to making it work. Bandimere Speedway would have never come close to making it if it hadn't been for John Jr. and the family. And even though you run slower because of the altitude, it's my favorite place to go race. The track is immaculate and everyone involved has done a tremendous job."

Dallas Gardner's heart pumped when he first saw the completed racetrack. Over 18 months earlier, he had delivered what could have been devastating news to the Bandimere family. But now, Bandimere Speedway was worthy of the title "Super Track" and became that coveted fan-friendly venue like Major League Baseball's Camden Yards in Baltimore, Maryland.

"This is beautiful!" Gardner thought. "This is a stadium!"

Longtime NHRA official Darrell Zimmerman assisted in the design and was especially pleased with the reaction that was coming from the racers.

"It's the only track with a downhill staging lane," he explains. "So when drivers stage their cars, they don't have to start the engine. They can put their car in neutral and coast down the hill. They just love that part. It helps them keep the engines cooler."

McMurtry appreciated how the renovation impacted the fans.

"The facility is absolutely unique because the spectators are looking down on the track with a commanding view," he says. "They're in the foothills and they have downtown Denver as a backdrop. On a nice clear day, the fans can see forever. It's really spectacular at night under the lights. It's just a pleasant place to go."

NHRA Funny Car championship racer John Force had enjoyed going to Bandimere Speedway long before it was renovated and reopened in 1989. But his entrepreneurial side couldn't help be impressed with the commitment that the family made to create one of drag racing's most spectacular settings.

"People don't understand, in this economy, how difficult it was for the Bandimere's to spend millions of dollars to cut away some of the mountain and make those improvements," Force says. "They weren't a wealthy family, but they invested and took a chance. Bandimere Speedway is beautiful. But it's beautiful because it wasn't built out of steel. It was carved inside of a mountain. You look at Mount Rushmore. That's how I compare Bandimere Speedway. I'm a race fanatic. I'm not only a racer and a champion, but I'm a fan of the sport. I'm a fan of the people that have grown the sport. That's why I'm a big fan of John Bandimere Jr. and the Bandimere family."

As the fans, racers, sponsors and NHRA officials took in the inspiring new accommodations, there was still some fuel to burn, some tires to turn, and some trophies to be earned. But first, the opening ceremonies set the stage for what would be an eventful weekend.

"Maybe it was being on the mountain, but it almost felt like a spiritual connection," Joe Hilger says. "It was great to see the crowd, along with Colorado Governor Roy Romer, and the various communities of people that were there to support the Bandimere family. Whether it was getting the facility done in time or the things that helped them build that track in the first place, you had this sense that there had always been a guiding light directing them every step of the way."

It was a Thursday night when the track's staple announcer and voice of Bandimere Speedway Bruce Kamada led Bandimere Jr., David Bandimere and Joanna Gager out to the starting line. There was a large piece of cloth draped over a post on the eastside of the starting line. When Kamada pulled back the covering, it revealed a street sign that said, "JOHN SR. BLVD: 1986 HB" or "John Bandimere Sr.: Heavenbound in 1986."

Bandimere Jr. then followed the unveiling of the touching monument that his staff had secretly organized for the siblings with a moving tribute to the racetrack's larger-than-life patriarchal figure.

"After all we'd been through, it was such an emotional moment," David Bandimere recalls.

To the naked eye, the rest of the Mopar Parts Mile-High NHRA

Nationals went off without a hitch. Gardner assumes it wasn't a perfect weekend from an operations standpoint, but he wasn't terribly concerned.

"It was really amazing," he says. "I'm sure there were things in that first event that we didn't even know about that didn't function as well as John Jr. and the family wanted them to. But we couldn't have asked for a better reopening of a racetrack that's been a flagship facility for us ever since."

That weekend, Joe Amato won the Top Fuel event, Bruce Larson took home the Funny Car title and Bob Glidden drove away with the Pro Stock prize. But more importantly to the drag racing community, Bandimere Speedway was back in the game.

As the Mopar Parts Mile-High NHRA Nationals were in full swing, David Bandimere sat at the north end of the property and basked in the panoramic view. He thought back to the many people that had given of their time and resource to help make it all possible. But his emotions overwhelmed him when he let his mind drift back to the very beginning.

"I remembered how it looked when I was a child," he says. "I remembered walking through those fields and dreaming together with my dad. I could hardly believe the transformation before my eyes. This was truly a gift from God."

It was, in fact, an emotional weekend for the entire Bandimere family. They understood the unusual sacrifices of working long hours throughout the week and during the weekends, and doing so together as a family, which often adds difficult dynamics that don't typically exist in the corporate world.

John Bandimere Jr. too found himself gazing out over the starting line from his perch in the tower with one overriding thought in his mind:

"To God be the glory. Great things He has done."

Rest For The Weary

At the conclusion of the 1989 Mopar Parts Mile-High NHRA Nationals, the contractors who had worked on the renovation came to Bandimere Jr. for the rest of their money. But due to the cancellation of the permanent loan, he was again short on cash. In as transparent fashion as possible, he explained to them the situation and assured them that he was working on a quick resolution to the problem.

Until that moment, Bandimere Speedway had never had a lien placed on them. But after the meeting, that number jumped from zero to 34. Bandimere Jr. knew the situation was precarious. It would only take two disgruntled lien holders to force him into involuntary bankruptcy.

Bandimere Jr.'s attorney reassured him that he could take care of the problem. But a few days later, he changed his tune and recommended that Bandimere Speedway file for Chapter 11 bankruptcy, get the money in order, and then pay off the contractors.

"There was no way I could do that," Bandimere Jr. says. "My father would roll over in his grave if he knew I had filed for bankruptcy. I didn't even want to use that word."

Instead, Bandimere Jr. took some time to "be quiet and listen to the Lord." From that prayerful consideration emerged the decision to visit with each lien holder and ask for a dollar amount that would allow him to settle the account. He also asked them for forgiveness. It was a very humbling experience.

After crunching the numbers, he realized that he was still short and needed to borrow $870,000. After learning that his bank, Jefferson Bank & Trust (JB&T), wouldn't be able to handle the total amount of the loan, he brought an unusual request to the President of JB&T, Moe Grotjohn. Bandimere Jr. had found a smaller bank that would handle the $870,000 at a favorable interest rate but wanted to be in first position. He wanted to know if JB&T would be willing to take second position. Grotjohn laughed. Not many banks, if any, would take second position to a smaller bank.

That same week, however, Grotjohn invited Bandimere Jr. to join his table at a Boy Scout breakfast held at the Pepsi Center in downtown Denver. During the event, Grotjohn turned to Bandimere Jr. and delivered some surprising news.

"The Board met last night and decided to take second position," he said.

Bandimere Jr. broke down in tears. He stepped away from the

table and immediately called his wife Lorraine. Together they rejoiced and thanked God.

"I guess they had faith in me," Bandimere Jr. says. "Actually, I think it was faith in God. There's no other way to explain it."

His jubilation was short-lived, however, as he realized once again that the numbers weren't adding up. This time, it was $100,000 that Bandimere Jr. was short. Desperate to remove the 34 liens against the speedway, he went to Kelso Kelly who was the President of Vectra Bank.

"Do you have any collateral?" Kelly asked.

"My signature," Bandimere Jr. meekly replied.

Kelly stepped away from his desk and returned a few minutes later with a check for $100,000 in his hand. The two signed the note and Kelly sent Bandimere Jr. on his way with one final piece of instruction. He would need the loan repaid in 90 days.

Once the money was secured, Bandimere Jr.'s attorney set up a date when the lien holders could collect their payments. Each one scheduled a time to meet with Bandimere Jr., his attorney and a notary at a neutral location that had been secured for the day. As they arrived one by one, Bandimere Jr. knew that they were still unhappy about the situation. But he didn't run from the uncomfortable circumstance. He sat there and thanked them for being patient and in some cases taking less than what was actually owed.

Bandimere Jr. left the room feeling like the weight of Thunder Mountain had been lifted from his shoulders. Now, he and his team back at the speedway had to get to work. The principal and interest payments that first year totaled $875,000. Until 1989, Bandimere Speedway had never shown a profit of more than $250,000 in a single season. But that year, the business sold $1.2 million in advertising. The substantial increase served as a testimony to the family's resilience and God's faithfulness to provide the extra needed income.

To this day, Bandimere Jr. contends that it was never a matter of money, but rather a matter of trust. The story brings to his mind a Bible verse found in Daniel 12:13:

"As for you, go your way till the end. You will rest, and then at the end of the days you will rise to receive your allotted inheritance." (NIV)

In that Old Testament passage, God was responding to Daniel's question about what he should do next. The faithful prophet was at a crossroads and was unsure of which direction to go. God's promise to Daniel resonated with Bandimere Jr. during the tumultuous circumstances at the racetrack.

"You don't have to worry about how it's going to end," Bandimere Jr. says. "God is in control."

16
Mile-High Memories

When Bandimere Speedway reopened for the Mopar Parts Mile-High NHRA Nationals in 1989, it was nothing less than a miracle. And even though the initial excitement of that historic weekend eventually dissipated into the notoriously thin air, the next several years still provided countless opportunities for the world's greatest drag racers to figure out how to beat the unusual atmospheric conditions on Thunder Mountain.

Altitude Check

Bandimere Speedway sits 5,800 plus feet above sea level, which is 520 more feet than in a mile. Those who drive regularly at higher altitudes get used to the car performance issues over time, but travelers and passer-bys might notice some not so subtle differences. That's because air becomes thinner as altitude increases and engines need air for combustion. Therefore, an average streetcar will lose about three percent of its horsepower for every 1,000 feet of altitude.

Supercharged engines certainly help combat some of that loss, but even the high-powered NHRA dragsters can drop 1.5 percent per 1,000 feet, which for competitors at Bandimere Speedway translates into roughly an 8.5 reduction. It's something the local racers have been dealing with from the beginning.

"Racing at a high altitude teaches you a lot about your car," Jim Head says. "You really have to struggle to make power. But when you figure it out, you can use it to your advantage at sea level and in other atmospheric conditions."

Mike Edwards admits that you "don't ever get it figured out," but he has had some success at the Bandimere Speedway nonetheless. He won a modified event there in 1981 and two Pro Stock championships at the Mopar Mile-High NHRA Nationals. Although no one has broken the 200-barrier yet in his division, Edwards was one of the first to log a round in less than six seconds, albeit in a testing session.

"The more you go and the more you run, you do get it better," Edwards says. "But it's such a challenging place. You never know what you're going to get with the weather. It can be super hot and it can be cooler at times. We've gotten faster and faster over the years."

Fellow Pro Stock champion Allen Johnson has especially fond memories of Bandimere Speedway. In 1996, Johnson was making his debut at the national level and traveled to 20 races including a much-anticipated visit to Denver where his car sponsor Mopar Parts was also the event's title sponsor.

"I couldn't wait to get there," Johnson recalls. "We had to borrow a lot of stuff from people the first time because we really weren't prepared for how different it was. The only thing that's the same about racing up there is the paint on the car and the driver."

Ironically, Johnson qualified for his one and only race that season and even managed to win the first round. Since that humble beginning, he has won five times at Bandimere Speedway including a hot streak of five out of seven events through the 2013 season.

"We just developed a combination there years ago that nobody else has done," Johnson explains. "The other cars have caught us a little bit, but we've just been ultra fast there. We worked really hard to get that setup because of our strong appreciation for Mopar and the Bandimere family."

Five years prior to Johnson's arrival, Lori Johns ran a 4.991 during a Friday-night Top Fuel qualifying run to become the first four-second driver at Bandimere Speedway. Dave McClelland announced that record-breaking time and many other milestones from his unique vantage point in the track's tower.

"I was always amazed that the cars were able to perform as well as they did at that altitude," he says. "I've done a little racing on my own and you can quickly realize the difference in altitude and atmospheric pressure. It's amazing to see how well those cars run up in the mountains, and it's a tribute to the Bandimere family for giving the racers a surface with such great traction to run on."

Former NHRA Competition Eliminator racer Ron Neff had the unique distinction of calling Bandimere Speedway his home track. In 1990, he won the Division 5 championship in a points competition that came down to the final race in Denver. Neff was also a three-time runner-up at the Mopar Mile-High NHRA Nationals (1987, 1990 and 1991).

When his son Clint Neff competed in Competition Eliminator at the 2011 national event, he was able to communicate with his father through a two-way radio device. After winning the final round and the prestigious championship, the younger Neff was overtaken with emotion.

"Dad, I love you," he relayed back to his proud father.

"The wins are exciting everywhere, but winning in Denver is a big deal because half of the crowd knows who we are," Ron Neff says. "We've been racing up there since we started and have such a great rapport with the Bandimere family. When I was still competing, I used to call Sporty and ask if I could make a couple of runs to test out a new clutch or something like that. He would meet me out there at night and turn the lights on. I'd make a couple of runs and then he'd shut the lights down and we'd leave. They've always treated us like family."

By the time Top Fuel championship driver Antron Brown entered the scene in 1998, Bandimere Speedway had fully developed into one of the nation's premier facilities thanks in part to the 1994 addition of the Top Eliminator Club. This 752-seat seating area includes a large tent on its 43-foot by 150-foot pavilion for hospitality events and gives spectators one of the sport's most unique vantage points as it sits angled next to the tower and overlooks the starting line.

Brown started his career in the Pro Stock Motorcycle division and placed second on three occasions at the Mopar Mile-High NHRA Nationals. He switched to Top Fuel in 2008 and through 2013 had won the event two times (2009 and 2012) and finished second once (2008).

"I've always been impressed with the track layout," Brown comments. "It's state of the art and the sites that surround it are like a painting that you're living in. What makes it really great is the Bandimere family. They are true blessings to our sport. They are always going the extra mile to take care of the racers and put on a great show for the fans."

But in some instances, the track provided moments for race fans and the community that transcended horsepower and burnouts and four-second runs. As Bandimere Speedway developed its business and outreach models, it created opportunities for special events such as concerts, running events, bicycle races, the Seventh Day Adventists' Camporee, and Easter sunrise services with special guests like former San Francisco Giants pitcher Dave Dravecky.

Then, there have been unplanned circumstances that brought an uncanny sense of calm amid the usually raucous sound of roaring engines and cheering fans. For NHRA Division Five Area Director Rob Park, there was one moment that stands out and will linger in his memory for years to come.

In July of 1999, the Mopar Mile-High NHRA Nationals were in the middle of a rain delay. Race officials were struggling to figure out how they were going to finish the event.

"We were feeling sorry for ourselves," Park remembers. We were burdening ourselves with the rain and what we were going to have to do in order to get the race completed."

Three months earlier, an infamous shooting took place roughly 10 miles to the southeast of Morrison at Columbine High School. Bandimere Jr. had invited a group of students from the school, including many who had been injured, to attend that weekend. Park was in race control when the students came in the room to visit with them. One of them was in a wheelchair. Another was on crutches. Park was captivated as they told their stories of survival.

"The rain suddenly became a very minimal hurdle for us to over-come," he says. "It put things in perspective. One kid told us how he played dead because his friend was lying next to him dead and bleeding. That's something I will never, ever forget. It was a life-changing experience for me thanks to the Bandimere family and the relationship they have with the community. They had the foresight to invite those kids and let them have a moment of relief and do something fun after being involved in something so tragic. I think about it all the time. Whenever I'm getting down, I remember that things could be a lot worse."

Winds of Change

By 1996, it had been 10 years since John Bandimere Sr.'s passing. During that time, Bandimere Speedway had weathered some incredible literal storms like the devastating winds that destroyed the eastside grandstands. The track also came through several figurative storms such as the legal battle with the Colorado Department of Transportation, the NHRA ultimatum, and the financial rollercoaster ride that ensued.

As the drag racing business grew, working together as a family was proving more difficult. John Bandimere Jr.'s family became more involved while David Bandimere's family and children were going in a different direction. While older sister Joanna Gager and her husband Rich had already pursued other interests years earlier, another inevitable change was on the horizon. The two brothers came together for a frank discussion about the future.

John Jr. and David were each fifty percent owners in Bandimere Speedway at the time and John was doing some personal estate planning. During this process, it became clear that they needed to make a decision as to who would be operating the track for the future. Given the fact that David clearly had the gift of ministry and John and his family were fully engaged in the racetrack, the day finally came when John Jr. took control of the track and his younger sibling moved into the next phase of his life. It was a difficult decision for both brothers because of their love and respect for each other.

Although Bandimere Jr. and his siblings have nothing but unconditional love for each other, the idea of working together long term was no longer a reasonable option.

"It wasn't always easy for David and I to work together," he says. "We didn't always see eye to eye. And that's especially tough when you're dealing with family members. But the Lord has helped us work past that and bring us to a place of peace and contentment within our relationship."

David admits that even after all these years he still misses his daily involvement at the track.

"It's been really difficult at times," he says. "I had always envisioned the family being like Knott's Berry Farm. I was with dad so much in the early years and I spent so much time with both he and my mom as they built this place from the ground up. It was bittersweet to move on, but it was for the best. The experience taught me that we should learn as early as possible to hold the things of this life very lightly. God may have something different and better in store."

The day that David Bandimere packed up his belongings and left the track was one of the hardest days of his life. It was a long time before he could drive past it on C-470.

"The racers are like family and the fans were a blessing," he says. "I tell people who ask me about the track that when they see it or pass by it they are witnessing a true miracle and gift of God."

Since then, David Bandimere, like his dad, John Sr., has enjoyed many interests. One of them has been taking the role of family collector and historian. He has also been blessed to take part in various ministries, business opportunities, and car-related activities.

Just like John Sr. and Frances, David and Barbara have worked and ministered together their entire married life. Through their various avocations involving marriage prep and the mentoring of couples and individuals, they have been a "safe" place for many that have crossed their paths.

David, like his brother, John Jr., enjoys speaking to groups and sharing not only family history, but also the power and blessing of leaving behind a legacy of faith.

Even though they haven't been involved at the track in nearly 20 years, Barbara Bandimere remains thankful for the experience of a lifetime.

"God really used each person in his or her own place," she says. "Each person had a unique role in how this got started. He used all of us, as we were willing. It was neat to be a part of that history—to see it develop and grow and to be used for whatever He wanted at the time."

But the amicable departure wasn't the only wind of change that was blowing through the valley. In fact, during that same year, Bandimere Jr., began exploring some intriguing options. Even though the business was secure, residential development was getting closer and there was a concern that this might become a problem with neighbors who did not understand their business.

A unique opportunity arose when a serious offer was made to buy the Bandimere Speedway property. When Bandimere Jr. signed that contract it opened the door for a conversation between landowners on highway I-70 past Denver International Airport to put in an oval track and drag strip.

That same year, Pikes Peak International Raceway was built just south of Colorado Springs. A young business leader named Rob Johnson was brought on as consultant for the track and two years later was hired as its president.

The Lehman Brothers investment firm out of New York was the majority of the Pikes Peak ownership group and was not terribly happy that there might be another oval track in the state providing unwanted competition. Although his bosses were actively lobbying against the new location, Johnson reached out to Bandimere Jr. in hopes of extending a personal olive branch. The two met for lunch.

"I didn't know if he was going to throw me out of the restaurant or not," Johnson jokes. "I was working for the people that didn't want him to have a new motorsports facility. I didn't know how it was going to go. But I quickly explained to him that I had no role in fighting the project. My only interest was in operating a motorsports facility. I was 29 years old at the time."

Johnson's fears were quickly alleviated.

"I believe you," Bandimere Jr. responded.

Instead of a rebuke that Johnson said would have been justified, Bandimere Jr. expressed his desire to get to know and act as a mentor for his younger counterpart.

"He was just wonderful to me," Johnson says. "It was an interesting start to our relationship. It told me everything about his character."

The plans for a new racetrack and the sale of land eventually fell through. Since then, the Bandimere family has seen God's hand of provision come through many times like it did with the construction of highway C-470, which has given the speedway tremendous exposure and also provides a much-needed noise buffer.

Another benefit to the situation was a newfound friendship between Bandimere Jr. and Johnson that emerged. The two came together to resurrect the Colorado Motorsports Hall of Fame, which had been dormant since the 1970s. Both men put money into the organization and brought a sense of pride and recognition back to the state's racing community. More importantly for Johnson, he made a lifelong friend whom he can go to for just about anything.

"I can call him anytime of the day and he'll always be there for me," he says. "And it's not just about motorsports. We've talked about family. We've talked about medical issues. We've talked about faith. That's just the kind of guy that he is."

Like God Coming Over That Mountain

Bandimere Speedway has seen its fair share of close calls and harrowing moments over the years. But until 1996, no one had died in a race-related incident. Bandimere employee and close friend Chuck Silva was working in the starting line area when a dragster backed up and fatally struck him.

The Bandimere family joined with the Silva family to create the Chuck E. Silva Memorial that resides in the pit area beneath the flagpoles. It is in that location where fans can order an engraved brick in honor of a person, event or memory that can be viewed by anyone who enters the facility. The Bandimere family also created the Chuck Silva Top Performer Award that is annually given to a racer who had an unprecedented year at the track.

A few years later, on August 18, 2003, Bandimere Speedway suffered its first driver fatality. Loveland native John Reynolds was in the Super Chevy event that night racing a 1991 Corvette ZR-1 Pro-Mod that he had transformed into a Nitro Coupe. The 49-year old racer had achieved a speed of 212 miles per hour, but when attempting to stop, his parachutes were entangled. Reynolds slammed into the net at the end of strip and the supercharger was ripped from the car and hurled through the windshield.

It was 12 years earlier, however, when a non-racing related death rocked the drag racing world. Businessman Joe Pisano (head of Linoleum Pistons) dove headfirst into the sport as an active owner, car chief and manufacturer. In 1991, Pisano was 63 years old and had a history of heart problems. He desperately wanted to compete at the Mopar Parts Mile-High NHRA Nationals despite his doctor's warning that the thin air could be detrimental to his health.

After watching his new driver Dave Pulde make a checkout run in the Pisano Olds Cutlass, he died in the arms of his crew in the tow vehicle on the return road.

"I lost a very good friend on that mountain," John Force says. "Joe Pisano was a guy that helped give me my start. I was in the pits when it happened. I've always said I'm going to be with the fans until I drop. And I thought to myself, 'If I'm going to die at a race-track, that would be the place to go–right on the side of God's mountain.' I've watched those clouds come over the hill. It's like God coming over that mountain.' That's how I feel about Bandimere Speedway."

In 1998, Force made history in Denver with the track's first run over 300 miles per hour. That Friday night his qualifying time was actually 301.70 and marked an important moment for the speedway. Ten years later, in 2008, the track celebrated its 50th anniversary and debuted a series of upgrades including an all-concrete racing surface, a newly paved shutdown area, new Musco lighting and an innovative cooling system placed underneath the launch pad on the starting line.

As impressive as those accomplishments might seem, Force will be the first to tell you that record speeds and hordes of trophies are insignificant memories in comparison to the enduring friendships that have developed over decades of time and the life-changing moments that are etched deep inside the heart.

"I've had nights where I stood at the edge of the mountain and cried," Force says. "I've gotten emotional when I thought I wasn't going to be able to race because of my injuries. I'm John Force. I'm not going to kid you. I don't know if I have the religion that John Bandimere has, but I believe in God, and I stood at the base of that mountain and I prayed with my family. I believe there's something there. The Bandimere family built that racetrack. Like Noah built the ark, I believe they built something there that God wanted them to build. It's unbelievable. I'm very emotional about that place."

17

Out In Front

For over 75 years, the Bandimere name has been associated with innovation. Even before John Bandimere Sr. was supercharging cars in the late 1930s, he was tinkering with tractor engines on the farm or thinking up new and more efficient ways to solve old problems in his speed shop. But the technical creativity didn't die with Bandimere Sr. in 1986. In fact, the mantle had already been picked up several years earlier albeit in a slightly different way.

John Bandimere Jr. admittedly did not inherit his father's mechanically inclined mind. He did, however, exhibit a significant level of business savvy that Bandimere Sr. lacked, and used that foresight to surround himself with people who could continue the family's innovative legacy.

Perfect Timing

When Bob Brockmeyer first attended a race at Bandimere Speedway in 1977, he was expecting to have a good time. He wasn't, however, expecting to develop a life-altering relationship with Bandimere Jr.

Over the next couple of seasons, Brockmeyer went from the stands to the strip where he competed in his 1970 Maverick. He started out in the Heavy class and eventually worked his way up to Super Pro.

"It was hardcore bracket racing, maybe even more than it is today," Brockmeyer says. "The people were serious about it. We went a couple of years before we won a round, but then we started winning a lot after that. John knew all of his racers, but the more we won, the more often we had to go to the tower to collect our checks."

During the 1983 season, Brockmeyer took some time off from racing to build a house in Silverthorne, a mountain community about an hour west of Morrison. At the time, he was working as a computer engineer for the mining company AMAX, Inc. Bandimere Jr. was aware of Brockmeyer's skill set and approached him one day with an intriguing question.

"Why don't you build a new timing system for the race track?"

Up until then, Chrondek was the standard timing system for drag racing. The company's simplistic clocks worked, in essence, like a speed trap that captured a car's miles per hour and relayed that information to the tower where the speed along with the elapsed time (E.T.) was communicated to a worker at the time slip booth that was handwritten on a time slip and handed to the racer after a completed run.

"In those early days, the worst part of a drag strip was the timing system," Bandimere Jr. says. "No information was printed out so there were many chances for human error. It was always an issue."

Bandimere Speedway was already ahead of its time by using a closed circuit TV that gave the workers at the time slip booth a visual of the clocks. But the system was still clunky and at times unreliable. That led Bandimere Jr. to invite Brockmeyer to his home for dinner where the two "basically drew it up on a napkin at the kitchen table."

The first step was to put together an automated computer system that would print up the time slips. Bandimere Jr. purchased the first IBM AT computer in Denver and commissioned Brockmeyer with the difficult process of interfacing the new unit with the old Chrondek clocks. He knew Bandimere Sr. briefly before his passing in 1986 and fondly remembers as the track's patriarchal inventor kept a watchful eye on his progress.

"Mr. Bandimere was always up in the tower and he was very interested in what we were doing," Brockmeyer recalls. "He wasn't sure if we needed it or not, but he found it very interesting."

By 1984, Bandimere Jr. and Brockmeyer partnered to officially create Compulink and worked tirelessly to perfect the system. After months of testing, Brockmeyer remembers the night it finally worked. It was 2 a.m., that evening and Bandimere Jr. was so excited that he jumped in the air and fell backwards in a moment of joyous celebration.

Over the next two to three years, Brockmeyer continued to make improvements. He added intermediate timers that included data collection points at 60 feet, 330 feet, an eighth of a mile and 1,000 feet.

"We started putting those numbers on the time slips and of course the racers just loved it," he says. "We were giving them more statistical information than they had ever received before. Chrondek laughed at us. They told us we didn't need a computer to do it. They said we were wasting our time. But a couple of years later, they quit laughing."

In 1987, Brockmeyer removed the old clocks and computerized the entire system. Outside track operators were somewhat curious about what he was doing but no one was able to buy into it because it was too expensive. In fact, Compulink was not originally set up for the purpose of selling the system to other tracks. But it didn't take long for them to realize it was something they needed.

"The racers demand that type of innovation," Bandimere Jr. says.

As Compulink's popularity grew, so did NHRA's interest. Local NHRA division director Darrell Zimmerman knew about it and started the conversation with Bandimere Jr. about running a divisional race using the system. And then Dallas Gardner decided to run the Mile-High NHRA Nationals with Compulink. That led to its debut in Phoenix and eventually to its national implementation.

"John was willing to let us use the track as our guinea pig," Brockmeyer says. "He knew we were going to have mistakes but he was willing to put up the time and money to help make it a reality. It never would have happened without John's support. Nobody else would have put up the money. I love technical challenges and John just wanted to be number one in drag racing and ahead of the field."

When Bandimere Jr. and Brockmeyer brainstormed a plan on that kitchen napkin, it included a projection of what the timing system might look like in 10 to 20 years. Amazingly, Compulink has followed that plan remarkably close. The system is now being utilized in tracks all across the United States as well as internationally in Canada, Japan, Australia, New Zealand, Finland, Caracao, Brazil and throughout Western Europe.

"Sometimes I joke with John that I'm going to whack him because he got me into this crazy business," Brockmeyer laughs. "I'm not sure if I'm happy or not."

Although Compulink was originally set up as a 50/50 ownership deal between the two men, Bandimere Jr. gave up his 50 percent to Brockmeyer because his time investment was so much greater than originally anticipated. The only thing Bandimere Jr. asked in return was that Bandimere Speedway would always be updated and on the sport's cutting edge.

"I planted the seed and Bob caught the bug," Bandimere Jr. says. But drag racing historians know better.

"John had the foresight to automate the timing systems and improve the accuracy," retired NHRA employee Wayne McMurtry says. "Compulink has made a major impact on the competition side of drag racing. John is the father of that. He didn't do the engineering, but he saw the talent in Bob and was willing to financially support his efforts."

All In The Family

In 1977, a 13-year-old kid named Larry Crispe inconspicuously entered the Bandimere family's life, but would go on to make an immeasurable impact on Bandimere Speedway and the drag racing world at large.

That summer, Crispe was working for a property manager to clean up an old greenhouse in preparation for a listing. At the same time (and unbeknownst to him), his second cousin Kaye Peterson was inquiring at the Bandimere offices about a possible job for Crispe at the track. Kaye's husband Frank Peterson, a mechanical genius much like John Bandimere Sr., owned Lakewood Manufacturing, a successful company that he still operates today.

Crispe would ride his bike to Peterson's place daily and absorb all of his knowledge about welding, machining and tooling. Crispe's presence was becoming a bit excessive and Kaye Peterson knew that a part-time job at the race track would keep the inquisitive boy out of their hair.

An employee named Jim Koch was tasked with the hiring

process, but after he and Crispe failed to connect, John Bandimere Jr. jumped in and cut to the chase with a brief yet productive conversation.

"Can you pick up trash?" Bandimere Jr. asked Crispe.

"Yes sir!" the teenager emphatically replied.

Crispe returned the next day and set out to prove his worth. His first job was to clean under the grandstands. Crispe crawled on his belly and picked up every piece of trash he could find. Not even cigarette butts could deter the young man from making a memorable first impression.

"He's a keeper!" Bandimere Jr. declared.

At the time, however, Bandimere Jr.'s daughter Johnna wasn't so convinced.

"Why did you hire that dirty little kid?" she once asked her dad.

Since that fateful day, Crispe has worked in almost every area at Bandimere Speedway. Ironically, one of the few things he hasn't done at the track is sell souvenirs, which happens to be his wife Johnna's responsibility. The two first showed mutual romantic interest three years after Crispe's arrival when she began selling auto parts at the speedway and Crispe was spending some time at the family's Rocky Mountain Performance Warehouse in Denver. Although Johnna would call Crispe to order parts for the store at the track, most conversations would quickly stray into non-business related topics.

In February of 1985, Johnna Bandimere and Larry Crispe were married less than 10 years from the summer the two met at the speedway.

"They always say you'll marry someone like your father or your grandfather," Johnna Crispe says. "I couldn't have married anyone more closely connected to what my grandfather was like. He is a chip off the block."

Crispe was only around for nine years before Bandimere Sr. passed away in 1986. But even in that relatively short period of time, the youngster gained invaluable nuggets of wisdom and knowledge.

"I always thought he was magical and bulletproof," Larry Crispe says. "John Sr. would be working on a project with great intent, but if someone stopped by to chat, he would stop everything he was doing to take time for that person. He had great insight into many subjects and you never left a conversation wondering how he felt. He always let you know right up front where he stood. You could take it or leave it. But you always wanted to take it and then come back for more."

As Crispe worked around the facility throughout his formidable years, Bandimere Sr.'s advice and guidance impacted many areas of his life. To this day, he often finds himself moving dirt, repaving the track surface, replacing light poles, taking care of electrical, plumbing and drainage issues, and building, rebuilding or fixing whatever needs to be fixed. In those moments, Bandimere Sr. often comes to mind.

"What would Grandpa do?" Crispe sometimes thinks to himself.

Crispe fondly remembers when the two spent days cleaning out what is now the Bandimere Speedway office building. What should have been a short process was stretched out in comic fashion as Bandimere Sr. reminisced for hours about every item that touched his hands.

"A lot of the stories stemmed from his auction finds," Crispe recalls. "He loved auctions and would buy items even if he had no idea how he would ever use it. He repurposed everything. He had such a sharp mind. Sometimes he seemed disorganized yet he could find whatever he needed at a moment's notice."

Bandimere Sr. also passed down some of his creative secrets including how to make his trademark rocker arm clips using a machine that he had built. Crispe can't help but get a little sentimental when he sees that clunky device sitting there in the garage by the track's finish line.

"It's big and heavy and in the way," he says. "But I appreciate the constant reminder of Grandpa. I loved learning from him. He was stern yet patient and he always intertwined what he was teaching me with a lesson of love."

For a period of time, Crispe worked elsewhere from the track including stints at Sundstrand, Denver University (in the Machine and Tool Research Department), and Martin Marietta. In 1988, he was hired for the first time as full-time at Bandimere Speedway where he served as the general foreman and contractor for the redevelopment and remodeling of the track. Crispe's current role is as

Facility Manager, but he feels like his most important responsibility is keeping the weighty Bandimere legacy in tact and continually moving it forward.

"Although the torches have been passed to the next generations, I still feel like I'm taking care of this establishment for Grandpa Bandimere," Crispe says. "Along with my parents, he was instrumental in teaching me how to work hard and how to turn nothing into something. Much respect is due him."

For many within today's NHRA community and the Denver drag racing scene, Crispe's presence on the circuit provides a glimpse of the track's legendary patriarch whom most of them barely or never knew.

Professional racer Jim Head had the brief privilege of being around Bandimere Sr. in the early 1980s, but it was long enough for him to appreciate the unique link between Grandpa Bandimere and his grandson-in-law.

"Larry is not from the same bloodline but he's definitely of the same mindset," Head explains "Anyone can invent things in their mind, but he invents them and puts them on the ground. The purists in the sport really like to put down a big number. That requires a prepared surface that's practically perfect. Larry understands that and strives for that. It's amazing what's come out of the Bandimere racetrack. It's mindboggling. Larry has no close second."

Crispe's list of drag racing inventions and innovations is nothing less than impressive. The Push Bar is a device that attaches to four-wheelers and is used to push cars off the track quickly.

Other advancements involve his specialty—track preparation and traction. For instance, the Traction Tire Rotator is a device that puts rubber on the track more efficiently and smoothly. It works in concert with the Scraper, a device that uses fire to heat up old rubber and a blade to remove the hot rubber from the track surface, and the Spray Rig that dispenses fresh traction compound.

"Larry is all about the racer," NHRA Pro Stock championship driver Mike Edwards says. "It doesn't matter if it's a top fuel racer or a bracket racer. He goes out of his way trying to help them. We used to go out there and test before the race and Larry would always be out there prepping the track and trying to get it the best he could.

You don't get that at most places. Plus he's just a great guy. He's not a Bandimere but it seems like he should be."

Perhaps none of Crispe's inventions have been praised more, however, than the cooling system that he installed at Bandimere Speedway. Embedded in the concrete launch pad, it circulates chilled water from a pair of 12,000-gallon underground tanks through over 15,000 feet of lines. The cooled area is 345-feet long and stretches from 40-feet behind the starting line and outward to 305 feet. The cooling system helps reduce track temperatures by between 10 to 25 degrees.

"It can be very miserable on a hot summer day with the sun beating down at 5,000 feet," former NHRA announcer Dave McClelland astutely notes. "You don't have any smog to buffer you like you have in California. That cooling device at the starting line is one of the smartest things I've seen. Hot tracks hinder good performance and although they have less power due to altitude, the cooling system provides the mechanics the opportunity to put as much power as they can into the car so the tires will still get good traction."

From a driver's perspective, Edwards wholeheartedly agrees with that assessment.

"It gets pretty hot up on the mountain in the summer time and Larry's device cools the track right down. It's just another thing the Bandimere family has done to make the experience better for everybody. It's better for the drivers. It's better for the fans. They're a step ahead of everybody."

Crispe is passing that innovative spirit down to his sons Cale and Cody who have become affectionately known throughout the drag racing world as "The Traction Twins." Together, they have sold their equipment across the country and have been hired to prep tracks all over the world including regular visits to the Middle Eastern nation of Qatar.

"Everything the family touches turns to gold," NHRA pro stock driver Allen Johnson says. "Everybody in the business pays attention to what they do."

NHRA top fuel championship driver Antron Brown is yet another prominent figure within the sport who greatly appreciates the Bandimere family's contributions.

"NHRA has benefitted so much from innovations like the tire machines, the cooling system, and the timing system," Brown says. "The Bandimere's have made our sport much more efficient and fan friendly to enjoy side-by-side racing."

McClelland believes it is the family's commitment to technologically advancing the sport that has benefitted not just Bandimere Speedway but racetracks operators and race fans everywhere.

"Drag racing can be a very elusive success story," he says. "John Bandimere Jr. has proven that you can do it. You can't stay in this business for 50 plus years and not be doing something right. 99 percent of that is treating the people well. He gives his spectators more than they anticipate. He treats the racers with respect. He provides a facility that's second to none. With those kinds of attributes, that's what leads to making a success. That's the greatest legacy you can have. It's a third generation family business that's still there and it's still growing."

18
What Matters Most

Surroundings don't always dictate the most logical outcome in a person's life. John Bandimere Jr. knows this to be true. Just like his father's love of cars didn't drive him straight into the parts business (he originally wanted to be a cattle farmer), his devout Christian upbringing did not produce an authentic relationship with God throughout his childhood and teenage years.

Although Bandimere Jr. was baptized at the age of seven, he admits that he went through the motions and was only following Christ on the surface. When he was 19 years old, he was working at the parts store and living in a room upstairs. His mother invited him to a revival meeting at a Baptist church.

"It was like the preacher was preaching directly to me," he remembers. "They were singing 'Just As I Am' during the invitation, but I resisted."

That night, Bandimere Jr. couldn't sleep. He was feeling heavy conviction from the words he had heard from the evangelist. The next night, he returned to the church and this time walked to the front of the building and asked Jesus to save him. His pastor was surprised. Bandimere Jr. had been actively involved in youth ministry at the church and was a good kid who had never gotten into trouble.

But on that night, his faith became real for the first time in his life. Soon thereafter he was baptized again and discovered a sense of purpose like never before.

That life-changing decision eventually led Bandimere Jr. to search out ways to reach young people like him that wanted to serve God but were struggling to break free from what he calls "the allure of the world."

For instance, as a young adult he coached youth sports and taught Sunday School at Rocky Mountain Lake Baptist Church where he worked with a small group of boys.

"I didn't know what I was doing," he admits. "I was just willing to do it."

One of his students was a kid named Danny Jackson. Years later, Jackson married a woman named Sandy whose father was Bandimere Speedway's bookkeeper and became the chaplain at Canyon County Penitentiary. Over the years, he has led thousands of inmates to Christ.

Jackson was one of many young people that Bandimere Jr. mentored along the way. His relational approach to evangelism carried over into the business world and his many friendships within the drag racing community.

Roger Guzman is among those whose life has been greatly impacted due to his friendship with Bandimere Jr. Guzman had grown up around Bandimere Sr. and was affiliated with a group of young men that hung around the parts store during the early days of Denver's drag racing scene.

In the late '90s, Art Ward had a business in east Denver called Gold Rush Auto Sales. Guzman was working at a Dodge dealership in Northglenn. Ward was fighting cancer and wasn't expected to live much longer. He called Guzman and asked him to join he and Bandimere Jr. at his office.

When Guzman arrived, he was surprised to see that Bandimere Jr. had set up the elements for communion–something he had only previously seen at church.

"It was very emotional for me," Guzman says. "It's hard for me to explain. I felt so much peace at that time and I know Art did too. You had to be there to understand. It was a very religious thing that John did. It made me feel very humble that John would do that for Art. I don't know anyone else other than a priest who would have done that. It was very moving."

Over the next several weeks, Guzman moved in with Ward and his wife and helped tend to his needs. Bandimere Jr. visited them often for fellowship and prayer. Their time together created a peaceful atmosphere for Ward throughout his last days.

Ward died on May 6, 1996, two months after taking communion with his close friends. After his body was cremated, a small portion of his ashes and flower petals were placed in the parachute of a Top Fuel car. At a special memorial service, Guzman ran the car down the track at Bandimere Speedway and released the parachute. It was a fitting tribute to one of drag racing's legends and a testament to Bandimere Jr.'s great respect for the sport's pioneers.

Spiritual Birthdays

Bandimere Jr. doesn't pay close attention to statistics and track records. He can certainly recall key moments in the speedway's history and he greatly appreciates any relevant information that highlights such notable achievements. But Bandimere is much more interested in keeping tabs on what matters most–the spiritual fruit that his family's business has produced.

To that end, he maintains a journal that lists the names of every person who has accepted Christ over the years as a result of his focus on relationships. Bandimere believes in divine appointments–moments in time that God orchestrates–and makes sure to write down the date of each conversion (or "spiritual birthday" as he calls it) to remind himself of that biblical principle.

February 9, 1972
Dave Howery can't tell the story without getting emotional. He had driven 70 miles from Fort Collins for a job interview with Bandimere Jr. While he was hoping to work at the speedway, the two instead met at the parts store on 1212 W. Cedar Avenue in Denver.

After some small talk and the unfortunate revelation that Bandimere Jr. wasn't looking to hire at the moment, Howery was unprepared for the direction in which their conversation suddenly turned.

"Do you know Jesus as your personal savior?" Bandimere Jr. asked.

"I had no idea what that was," Howery now says. "The job application asked about my religion and I put down that I was Lutheran because that's how I was raised. But I had no idea what he was talking about."

"Do you remember ever seeing that picture of Christ knocking on a door?" Bandimere Jr. continued.

The image immediately came to Howery's mind. He had seen it inside an old Bible when he was a child.

"You have to open the door so He can come in."

"I folded right there," Howery says. "I got on my knees and asked Jesus to save me."

Remembering that moment ushers in a wave of emotion. After pausing to regain his composure, Howery then laughingly remembers how the interview concluded and the message he relayed to his wife who was back home.

"Well, I didn't get the job. But I got Jesus!"

Bandimere Jr., who remembers the exact time Howery accepted Christ (it was 3:45 p.m.), is still amazed when he thinks back to such an unlikely conversion story.

"Sometimes when we share the Lord with somebody, we kind of marvel that they're so ready," he quips.

Bandimere Jr. later found out that Howery's wife had organized a prayer meeting and an entire church was praying that he would accept Christ while traveling to Colorado. He eventually *did* get a job working at the Rocky Mountain Performance Warehouse where he befriended David Bandimere and later worked as salesman for the company. But that opportunity paled in comparison to how a job interview changed his life forever.

December 12, 2008

Dave Jackson was struggling with his insurance business. It just so happened that Bandimere Jr. was one of his clients. But his relationship with the track operator dated back to the 1970s when he attended races as a high school student and continued throughout the 1980s as a racer and later through his daughter's involvement in the speedway's junior dragster program.

It wasn't uncommon for Jackson to call Bandimere Jr. for advice. He trusted his judgment and appreciated his consoling spirit. But during this particularly rough patch, Jackson did something out of the ordinary. He picked up the phone and reached out to Bandimere Jr. at 12:15 in the morning.

"John talked to me about where I was with the Lord," Jackson says. "He led me to the point where I was ready to become a born again Christian. That phone call changed my life."

The next afternoon, when Jackson returned to his office after being away for a while, he found a Bible on his desk. Bandimere Jr.

had told his track chaplain Ken Webb about the phone call and how Jackson had committed his life to Christ. Webb then drove 60 miles from Morrison to Loveland and hand delivered the Bible.

"I wasn't even here," Jackson says. "But that's just how John and his people are."

Jackson will also never forget the day his son-in-law proposed to his daughter on the starting line at the track in front of 30,000 people. It was just another example of how Bandimere Jr. and his family had helped create a lifelong memory for a friend.

"He's just a genuine, great individual," Jackson says. "I've never known anyone like him. His compassion for people and his sincerity is extraordinary. It's amazing how he treats people. He practices what he preaches. He lives it."

December 22, 2008

Mitch Mustard was the stereotypical drag racing fan that frequented Bandimere Speedway during the '70s. He turned his love of the sport into a serious racing hobby of his own and later as a supporter of his daughters' junior racing careers and as a track sponsor.

Mustard's father did business with Bandimere Sr., so the relational progression between he and Bandimere Jr. was natural, although he first became friends with Sporty Bandimere and Larry Crispe.

"John would come up to the drivers in the staging lanes and welcome them and wish them luck," Mustard says. "As a promoter, that was his job but he went out of his way to express his love for you."

In 2007, Mustard bought a car from a man in Pennsylvania who was fighting stage-four throat cancer. He won a seven-round national bracket event the first time he raced the car. At the same time, Mustard had befriended the man (his name was Jim) and stayed in touch until his death a year later.

Mustard found out about his friend's passing while driving to Las Vegas where he was competing for a Super Gas divisional title. At that race, he had great reaction times and performed exceptionally well in two separate divisions (Super Gas and Super Comp).

"I felt like Jim was on my shoulders riding with me," Mustard says.

Mustard went on to win the Super Comp event in Las Vegas and then traveled to Pomona where he raced deep into the late rounds of the Super Gas division. When he got back to Colorado, he was dealing with a lot of emotions from the experience and went to talk to Ken Webb at the track on a weekday.

Webb wasn't in the office at the time, but Bandimere Jr. recalls that Mustard "just kept hanging around."

"Mitch, is there something I can help you with?" Bandimere Jr. inquired.

"Well, I just need to talk," Mustard responded.

After Mustard explained what he had been feeling, Bandimere Jr. invited him into his office to talk about it. He had shown up to talk to someone else but now realizes it was a divine appointment that God had orchestrated on his behalf.

"John told me that what I was feeling was the Holy Spirit talking to me," Mustard says. "He explained some things to me about Christ that I thought would be a big challenge but it turned out that they weren't. John led me to Christ that day."

On Thanksgiving Day in 2013, Mustard suffered a severe heart attack. It took two discharges from the defibrillator paddles to revive him. While that maneuver revitalized his physical heart, he and Bandimere Jr. both know that his eternal heart was saved five years earlier on yet another spiritual birthday.

December 21, 2009

It was a year after Bandimere Jr. had led Dave Jackson and Mitch Mustard to the Lord on those two memorable December days. As those relationships blossomed, he routinely stayed in touch with both men. So it wasn't a big surprise when Jackson called Bandimere Jr. at 5:05 p.m., on December 21, 2009.

But this time was different. Jackson wasn't calling to talk about his spiritual wellbeing. He was calling on behalf of his wife Denise who in fact was also on the line. She had seen her husband's transformation and was looking to experience that for herself.

Over the course of a few minutes, Bandimere Jr. prayed with Denise and led her in a prayer of salvation. It still brings him to tears when he reflects on how two phone calls then resulted in an entire family accepting Christ.

Influencing the Influencers

John Bandimere Jr. didn't set out to become a recognized businessman throughout Denver and its surrounding areas, nor did he anticipate that running a race track would allow him the opportunity to pour into the lives of hundreds of aspiring leaders.

But that's exactly what has happened over the past 40 plus years.

Rod Olson isn't surprised. He has seen firsthand how key components such as faith, family, and integrity have allowed Bandimere Jr. to reap the benefits of such a well-respected platform.

"He reminds me so much of Andy Griffith," Olson says. "He is a simple man in a complex world. He's been able to live for Christ and not get caught up in a world that sometimes lacks authenticity. He is genuinely authentic. What you see is what you get. He's also a warrior for the Lord. He's courageous and steadfast."

Olson was a college football coach for 20 years. Then his life changed about 15 years ago when he was taught how to coach using biblical principles. In 2003, Olson's book *Legacy Builders* established him as a leading authority on Christ-centered coaching. Bandimere Jr. saw a need within the coaching world and invited Olson to Denver for a meeting. From there, Bandimere Jr. was instrumental in the creation of Fellowship of Christian Athletes Coaches Ministry and the hiring of Olson as its first director. Olson has since relinquished the reins and now operates his own ministry called Coaches of Excellence, but the impact of his work with FCA continues to grow.

"If it wasn't for John, I don't think FCA would be where they are not just in Colorado but across the nation," Olson says. "He pushed the idea of coaches ministry before anyone was doing it."

Olson's move to Colorado also opened the door to a relationship with the late Colorado Rockies president Keli McGregor and then team manager Clint Hurdle. Olson mentored McGregor up until his death in 2010 and has continued in that role with Hurdle even after he was let go by the Rockies and eventually hired by the Pittsburgh Pirates.

Not long after Olson's first book was published in 2003, Bandimere Jr. began hosting a Bible study at the track for Denver area CEOs. Early participants included Joe Coors Jr. from the famous Coors family, Tom Honig, Regional President of Mountain Midwest Operations for Wells Fargo, Shawn Caldwell, chiropractor for athletes on the Denver Broncos and Colorado Rockies teams, and the aforementioned McGregor. About eight to 12 people attended early on. Over time, that number has grown to roughly 16 with a total impact of over 30 that sporadically attend.

Another regular attendee has been a man who works for the Drug Enforcement Agency (DEA). He once jokingly suggested that he and Olson should do a link analysis much like the DEA conducts when attempting to "follow the money" during a crime investigation. Only in this case, the purpose would be to track the successful ministry opportunities that have been launched out of that influential group.

"It is absolutely crazy all the people that I've been allowed to touch, by the grace of God, because they were in that room," Olson says. "John was instrumental in that. He has an ability to prepare people and link people. He probably has 150 guys like me that he mentors and talks to on a regular basis. He's a legacy builder and he continues to build legacy in other people. His footprint is pretty large."

Mitch Mustard began attending the Bible study for racers after he accepted Christ in 2008 and has gladly made the most of those monthly meetings.

"Without John, I wouldn't have been able to talk about spiritual things," he says. "He has been a very trustworthy mentor that I can go to and learn more about Christ. He has become a very close friend."

According to Colorado Christian University president Bill Armstrong, Bandimere Jr. provides business leaders and those around him with a shining example of "what it is to be a Christian in everyday life."

"A lot of people are Christians on Sunday and act one way when they go to church and then when they get out into the real world, they act completely differently," he opines. "John is a role model for what it means to be a follower of Jesus in the world of business. He's authentic. He wears his faith on his sleeve. It's not in an odd sense but in the most natural, normal kind of way. I appreciate that."

And because of his platform as a track operator and a successful businessman, Bandimere Jr. has influence over others in ways that, as Armstrong explains, might not always be visible.

"What John does in effect by honoring Christ in that way is he gives permission to people around him to do the same–people who don't have his standing and aren't as prominent in business and aren't as well known and aren't as mature and aren't as poised and confident as he is. Because he is faithful in his commitment to Jesus, he makes it easier for other people around him. I think that is terribly important."

In his teaching materials, Olson often asks the question, "Who is on your Mount Rushmore?" In other words, who are the four people that have had the greatest impact on your life?

"John Bandimere is on my Mount Rushmore," Olson confidently states. "I can always call on him as a mentor and as a friend. I know he's going to speak truth into my life. He's not going to tell me what I want to hear or how to help my career. He's going to tell me what I need to know as a follower of Christ and a father and a husband. There's no amount of money I can put on that."

19

Mountainside Missionaries

Onlookers haven't always understood why the Bandimere family has invested so many years and so much money into a drag strip. After all, in those early days, drag racing wasn't the most reputable activity in Denver or anywhere else in the country.

But the family's passionate pursuit of serving the racing community makes more sense when you understand the original purpose behind Bandimere Speedway and how that purpose has evolved and grown over time. The track has always been and continues to be a platform and a mission field. It started with John Sr. and his unique evangelism method.

"Our family heritage is a dual love affair," David Bandimere says. "Our dad had a love affair with the Lord and he had a love affair with performance and cars. Our mom embraced that. She was as much a hot rodder on the street as he was. They were a perfect match. They loved the Lord and loved life and loved cars. People were drawn to them."

And while the track has changed dramatically since 1958, the family's commitment to making a spiritual impact on the community has never wavered.

In The Public Eye

Accidents don't happen at every race, but they certainly are not an uncommon occurrence. At one particular event, a driver lost control of his car and wrecked. While the emergency responders were attending to the injured racer, John Bandimere Jr. sat down in front of the public address system microphone and informed the sizeable

Friday night crowd that he wanted to take a few moments to pray for the driver.

For one fan, this seemed to be a curious moment.

"Are we at a church service?" he sarcastically inquired of a man sitting nearby.

"You know what?" the other man answered. "If you come to Bandimere Speedway, that's what you're going to get."

"That's cool," the seemingly satisfied patron responded.

People in the Denver area have known about the family's faith for years. It has been publicly acknowledged and routinely expressed at every level of competition. But when the NHRA began running national events at Bandimere Speedway in the late 1970s, the family's Christian beliefs came to the attention of the national drag racing scene. And nothing since then has changed.

"They pray before all of their races and when ESPN is there they still pray before races," Rod Olson says. "They are consistent in what they believe and God has blessed them because of that. John is a guy that everyone in the city can go to and can say he does it right."

An especially compelling moment presented itself during the 2012 Mopar Mile-High NHRA Nationals in the wake of the Aurora theatre shooting that had taken place just days earlier. Racer's For Christ (RFC) president Larry Smiley says that the community "was very tender" and still experiencing aftershocks from the tragic event.

On the opening Friday night, Bandimere Jr. asked Smiley if he would accompany him to the starting line and say a special prayer for the victims and their families. Just before pro qualifying, Bandimere Jr. said a few brief words and then handed the microphone to Smiley.

"It was just me and him out there," Smiley remembers. "It was hard to pray. I was choking up. Yet the Holy Spirit gave me a prayer. John and I hugged and walked off the track. We both had tears in our eyes because it was such a healing time. It was very powerful. I don't know of any other track that would invite the chaplain to invoke God's blessings on a hurting community. That night was really special."

At the end of the prayer, the respectful crowd burst into cheers.

Today, it remains one of Smiley's favorite moments in his 17-year history with RFC and yet another example of how the Bandimere family has gracefully allowed their Christian witness to shine through.

"We're not trying to force our beliefs on anyone," Sporty Bandimere says. "We just take the opportunities as they come. We always want to be willing to share and willing to step out and use the business as a platform for our faith."

For over 35 years, that has resulted in a naturally symbiotic relationship between Bandimere Speedway and RFC. Not only has the Bandimere family financially supported the ministry, Bandimere Jr.'s daughter Tami Shrader has spent time on the Board of Directors for the Christian Motorsports International, Inc., family of ministries that includes Team RFC.

"They are generous in so many ways," Smiley says. "They support us with our golf tournament every year. We were having trouble with our sound system a few years ago. At the end of the Mopar Mile-High NHRA Nationals, John asked me what it was going to take to get a new sound system. I gave him a number and he said 'Okay.' In a few weeks, he had sent me a check and we were able to get a new sound system. It wasn't surprising, but it was certainly very much appreciated. That's just how they are."

Smiley has been attending the event since 2001. Each time he arrives at the track, he can expect to get a hug from Bandimere Jr. that often ends with the two praying for each other. But according to Smiley, Bandimere Speedway stands out for another reason as well.

"This track is different," he explains. "When you arrive at the property, you can feel the difference. This track is prayed over every day. You can feel the presence of God through the power of those prayers. The heart of the Bandimere family is to honor God in everything they do because of their dedication to Jesus Christ."

RFC hosts a Sunday morning chapel service at all NHRA events, but the Mopar Mile-High NHRA Nationals are typically one of the most attended. During his 13-year history at Bandimere Speedway, Smiley says the gathering is always standing room only with over 200 people crowded underneath a large tent.

"I'll usually look out there and see the Bandimere family standing in the back or to the side because they didn't get there early enough because they're taking care of the race track," he says. "When I present the Gospel, we have so many hands that go up because we invite the fans to come in to chapel and the Bandimere's encourage that. I know that the family has interceded for that service and for that invitation, specifically that lives would be changed. God is there and God has been invited there. God has been encouraged to change lives and it just happens day in and day out through the life giving words of John and all of the family. That's what they do and that's who they are."

Smiley also recognizes the spiritual burden that Bandimere Jr. has for the racing community. He has seen firsthand how the popular track owner interacts with drivers and their crews when attending NHRA events outside of Denver such as in Pomona, Las Vegas and Phoenix.

"John has such a love for the racers," Smiley says. "He prays for them every day."

Perhaps that's why so many notable NHRA stars gravitate towards Bandimere Jr. and his family.

"They are pretty special folks to me and my wife Lisa," NHRA championship Pro Stock driver Mike Edwards says. "It's a pretty tough world out there, but John's not afraid to step right up to the plate. No matter who it is, John will tell it like it is and what he stands for. I respect him for that."

Throughout much of his career, Edwards has been affiliated with a ministry to teenagers called Young Life, and has appreciated the commitment Bandimere Jr. has to that program both nationally and in Colorado.

"John has always gone out of his way to get the Young Life kids out to the track on our Thursday night events," Edwards adds. "And he's always been there anytime I needed help. John is always willing to come pray with me. He's grounded. He's read the back of the book. He knows that drag racing has been good to him, but he sees the big picture. John is a tremendous witness out there for a lot of people to see."

Allen Johnson, also an NHRA championship Pro Stock driver, concurs.

"I look up to John because of his faith and everything he does from a Christian standpoint," he says. "I really look up to him and respect him for that. He really highlights that in everything he does. I need someone like that to guide me and give me inspiration."

And for Top Fuel championship driver Antron Brown, the Bandimere family represents a vital element within the sport.

"It's very important to have a family like the Bandimere's who aren't afraid to show their faith in God," he says. "They're out there smiling and letting other people know what is truly first in their life. It shows through their example and it shows people why they do what they do."

Most of the season, however, the Bandimere influence is primarily felt within the local community of drag racers. Veteran drivers like Butch Salter are among the many Denver-based enthusiasts who have been positively impacted by John Jr. and his naturally public faith.

"I've always admired him for his stand," Salter says. "He's always kept his faith. He's a good Christian man and he doesn't mind sharing it with anyone. There are a lot of people that have a problem with that and might have a grudge against the family, but I have nothing but praise for John."

Those closest to Bandimere Jr. are quick to point out the role his wife Lorraine has played throughout the years of living out his faith in the public eye.

"John is always out front, but that lady keeps him grounded," Rod Olson says. "It's a team effort. They made a commitment years ago to grow together. John has gone through a lot at the track and there's no way he could have made it through the challenges without her by his side."

And part of that package deal is a reciprocal appreciation that a diverse group of people shows for Bandimere Jr. and his wife.

"Everyone loves John and Lorraine," Olson says. "When you go to the races, there are all these different demographics of people. They can walk in all those different worlds and do it well. And they all love them both. That's a great testament to the anointing that they are walking in."

No Bull Jive Religion

John Force has known John Bandimere Jr. for nearly 40 years. During that time, Force has kept a watchful eye on his good friend from Denver. It's something that the legendary NHRA Funny Car driver often does, in fact, when a popular sports figure or celebrity starts to talk publicly about their Christian faith. Tim Tebow, for instance, is an iconic athlete that Force has closely followed since he burst into the nation's consciousness during his days as a Heisman Trophy winning quarterback from Florida.

While Force contends that the jury is still out on Tebow, he is convinced that he has a definitive judgment call when it comes to the Bandimere family's authenticity.

"They have a lot of religion," he says. "I'm not talking about the bull jive, but the real deal. When you stand at a race, we have the National Anthem. We have prayer. We have Racers For Christ. But the Bandimere family goes beyond that because they live it. They don't make it part of a show. You see that a lot in this day in age. But the Bandimere family is for real."

Part of Force's assessment is based on his observations of Bandimere Jr. throughout a wide array of financial realities. When they first met, the family was moderately successful, but by no means among the upper crust of Denver's wealthy elite. Force saw the Bandimere's fight for everything they had and trust God every step of the way.

"I cannot say one thing bad about the Bandimere family," he says. "I watched John Bandimere to see if money ever changed him. When the economy collapsed, nothing changed. He moved ahead. It's real easy for people to be great when things are going good. You find out the value of someone's greatness when they go through hard times and they don't change. That's what I see in the Bandimere family."

It's not to say that their relationship hasn't been tested. Force recalls a troublesome situation that arose leading up to one of the more recent Mopar Mile-High NHRA Nationals. The popular driver stays extremely busy appearing at car shows and sponsor-related activities in addition to promotional events at the various NHRA tracks. But this year, due to his overload, he told his promotions director to let Bandimere daughter Tami Shrader know that he wouldn't be able to participate in his usual slate of appearances.

"I struggled with that decision for months," Force confesses. "When I got to Denver, I went up to Tami and I had all of this guilt inside of me. After I apologized for my failure, I waited to get chewed out. I just knew that she was going to tell me how I'd let them down and now I was not going to get any of the favors I had asked for in the past."

But instead, Shrader gave the burdened driver a hug.

"You did nothing wrong," Shrader told Force. "We ask too much of you sometimes and you were just doing your job."

In an ironic turn of events, Shrader was essentially apologizing to Force in the midst of his own mea culpa.

"I was just amazed that I was the one that carried the guilt and yet there was never a problem," he says. "She really truly understood. Most promoters would have taken advantage of me in that moment. But not the Bandimere family."

When Force stood up at the 2013 season ending awards ceremony and accepted his 16th NHRA championship, he made an unusual statement.

"John Bandimere wants to see me saved," he told the audience while locking eyes with his longtime friend.

In that moment, Force harkened to his first experience at Bandimere Speedway and the kindred spirit he found in Bandimere Jr. Both men came from humble beginnings and worked hard to find a prominent place within the drag racing community. But Force is honest enough to recognize one stark difference.

"I've always believed in God, but I haven't always followed the Lord's hand," he says. "Both John and my wife have helped me down the road. When I was in the hospital after my accident in 2007, I thought a lot about the things that John has told me about God and why I've struggled to find Him in my own way. Every time we meet at the race, we have a chat. I'm getting better."

Just as Force has watched Bandimere Jr. over the years, the tables turn during the Mopar Mile-High NHRA Nationals when Bandimere Jr. observes Force each time one of his daughters gets

into a race car. As they speed down the track, Force watches intent-
ly for the chutes to come out and for the cars to come to a halt.

*"Thank you," he says under his breath before racing down to the fin-
ish line.*

"The relationship I have with John Force is special," Bandimere
Jr. says. "Life is filled with relationships and people don't always
understand that. It makes me cry when I talk about it, but that's what
God wants in our lives. He wants a relationship. Knowing all about
God is one thing, but *knowing* God is what's important."

God's Property

There's no way around it. Bandimere Speedway cannot stay
open if it is not financially viable. That's the harsh reality of modern
economics. Therefore, turning a profit is a significant priority. It isn't,
however, the number one priority. Bandimere Jr. recognizes the fact
that the track has a much higher purpose than securing his family's
future and that purpose goes back to his father's mission in life.

"All of this has happened because it was God's plan," he says.
"Our dad instilled a passion in us to not give up. That's why we're
still here today."

Longtime Racers For Christ president Larry Smiley astutely
notes that Bandimere Speedway is "much more than a race track. It's
God's property."

Retired Pennzoil and Shell executive Doug Miller spent many
years sponsoring events on that divinely inspired parcel of land. He
has continually been amazed at how the Bandimere family has managed to stand out in a world that typically does not convey traditional family values.

"Racing is not perceived as the most moral sport there is," Miller
explains. "Fast cars. Hot women. Shiny chrome. That doesn't exactly personify the Christian lifestyle. But John Sr., and John Jr., and the
entire family have been able to maintain their faith and make a successful business underneath that umbrella. Their faith permeates in
everything they do."

And that means never being afraid to let others know what they
believe and publicly acknowledging the inspiration behind everything they do.

"We run events and race and that's cool," Sporty Bandimere says. "But ultimately this is God's business. God is using us as missionaries on this mission field."

Bandimere Jr. readily admits that the family has had its fair share of problems. It's impossible to have a family business and not struggle at times.

"But we don't close the door and walk away," he adds. "You have to work it out."

And that willingness to work through the common issues that make a family business much more different than a corporation is what has allowed them to fulfill the plan that was set into motion over 55 years ago.

"Mom and dad would be most thrilled if they saw all of the opportunities we've had to impact God's Kingdom," David Bandimere says. "As a family grows, it's amazing how many lives the Lord lets you touch as a group. Two people fell in love and had these interesting passions. It's amazing to see what comes through that over the next generations. That's what it means to pass on a legacy and to have a godly heritage."

20

The
Bandimere Way

For Bandimere Speedway, the 2013 race season was especially significant. It marked 55 years since John Bandimere Sr. first broke ground on the property back in 1958. That same season provided another monumental milestone with the 35th running of the Mile-High NHRA Nationals and 25 years with Mopar as the event sponsor. In both instances, the Bandimere family was able to look back at a series of miraculous events that allowed them to overcome a slew of challenging obstacles.

Most of those scenarios have been chronicled throughout the pages of this book. All of them point back to the family's steadfast belief in one of their patriarch's favorite Bible verses.

"And we know that all things work for the good of those who love Him, who have been called according to His purpose." – Romans 8:28 (NIV)

"John Jr. had the capability of selling that property and living happily ever after," former NHRA president Dallas Gardner says. "I know that had to be a temptation. But I'm sure that one of his considerations was his family. His whole family works there and they always have. I think out of love for his family and loyalty to them, that's part of why John did what he did. It turned out to be a blessing to him and his family."

Bandimere Speedway has also turned out to be a blessing to countless others throughout the greater Denver area and throughout the state of Colorado. The track's impact has even been felt across the country and across the globe thanks to the innovations that have been birthed on the side of that mountain.

Many have wondered how the Bandimere family has managed to stay there despite growing concerns from the neighboring town of Morrison on one side of the mountain and the surge of housing developments on the other side. The equation is really quite simple if you ask those who know the family best: the investment of resources plus the investment into relationships equal the kind of returns that can never be measured by finite numbers or material success.

Resourceful Investments

Resourcefulness has taken on different meanings throughout Bandimere Speedway's existence. For Bandimere Sr., it was all about making the most of what was in his hand. He was notoriously tight with money and did everything within his ingenious mind to repurpose, recycle and reuse whatever precious materials he could find.

But Bandimere Jr. took over the track with a businessman's mentality. Early on, he and his brother David knew it would never survive on sporadic heads-up bracket racing. It was also clear that they would have to implement a new model for generating and dispensing resources.

John Force has observed that shift and has likewise taken a similar approach to his racing career.

"The Bandimere family isn't afraid to spend money," he says. "They aren't afraid to promote. In this day and age, everybody wants to pull back, but you've got to spend money to make money. You've got to tell the people you're there. You've got to educate them until you build a happening. That's what Bandimere has now. Every year, the pros will come and the fans know they're going to get a show."

For Denver-based enthusiasts like Mitch Mustard, there's an equally strong appreciation for how the family's financial commitment to the track impacts the local drag racing community.

"Most racetracks make money but don't reinvest it," he explains. "But John is always reinvesting the money he makes back into the track. He's made it a nicer facility. John is always doing things to make it a better experience for the racers and their wives and their kids. It's all about family."

Bandimere Jr. has also proven resourceful through an increasingly steady flow of diverse events that dot the speedway's calendar. The tracks hosts local races, divisional races, high school programs, junior dragster programs, testing and tuning opportunities, corporate events, concerts and holiday events. In other words, as Dallas Gardner notes, it's what Bandimere Speedway does the rest of the year, apart from the Mopar Mile-High NHRA Nationals, that makes the place successful.

"John realized that he had the opportunity to do a lot of other things based around drag racing and even other types of events besides drag racing," Gardner adds. "He has one of the fullest calendars. There's always activity there. There are a lot of track operators that don't think they have to work as hard anymore once they get a national event. But it's a tough business and John has figured out a way to attract more people to his facility."

Former NHRA driver and Colorado native Ron Neff knows firsthand what a thriving drag strip has meant to the area.

"The track has brought in thousands of people," he says. "It's helped build hotels. It's a big draw for the metro area. People now know where Morrison, Colorado is. That mountain has its own allure. To me, it's still *the* sporting event of Denver. Drag racing still has a lot of roots in Denver and that helps keep it going."

If it weren't for arthritis, Neff claims that he would still be driving today. But his retirement from the sport hasn't stopped him from getting excited every time he drives to the racetrack.

"When I take the exit off of Highway C-470, I'm surprised I don't get picked up by a policeman," Neff laughs. "It's almost like you're accelerating downhill and you can't wait to get there. I still get the goose bumps on the back of my neck."

Former track sponsor Doug Miller refers to Bandimere Speedway as "a landmark" and ranks it as one of Denver's most significant historical sites along with the Coors Brewery, the Molly Brown house and the Governor's mansion. Rob Johnson concurs and considers the Mopar Mile-High NHRA Nationals "an absolute advertorial for Colorado."

"The view on TV paints such a spectacular portrait of the state," he says."

Force takes his admiration a step further and considers how another significant investment might benefit drag racing.

"If NHRA ever sold, I wish the Bandimere family would buy it," he boldly states. "There's a principle that John Jr. has taught his family based on God's teachings that his dad taught him. I believe that doing good is what will deliver results. I'm starting to sound like a preacher, but no matter how much pain and suffering you go through along the way, I do believe that God has a plan. I really believe that."

Relational Investments

When Doug Miller first met John Bandimere Jr., he was a teenager hanging around the track and immersing himself into the car performance culture that John Bandimere Sr. had meticulously cultivated throughout the Denver area.

Bandimere Jr. was inconspicuously running the family parts store at the time and not nearly as prominent in the community. Over the course of many years, Miller has observed something telling about the retailer turned track operator.

"I'm sure John has had plenty of bad days," he explains. "I'm sure there are things that have upset him and made him mad. But probably more than anybody I know, he never allows anyone to see that. He's always got a smile on his face. He's always quick to compliment people. His faith as a Christian shows through in every part of his life."

There's no doubt that Bandimere Jr.'s business sense has elevated the speedway to unprecedented heights and carried the business through one harrowing venture after another. But if you ask anyone who has ever dealt with the man on a personal or professional level, you'll hear every single one convey a similar sentiment.

"John is a very astute businessman," former NHRA announcer Dave McClelland says. "He uses his knowledge of the business and the purpose he has in mind very intelligently. But the real reason for his success is all about how he treats people. He treats people like he'd like to be treated—with great respect and dignity."

This is first and foremost important when it comes to the family's relationship with the neighboring town of Morrison as well as the rapidly expanding housing developments that sit just across the other side of Highway C-470. With homes worth over $1 million within earshot of the track, many are awestruck when trying to understand how Bandimere Speedway has been able to stay in its current location.

"How do you think John Bandimere Jr. has been able to keep a drag strip right in the middle of Morrison with all of those houses around it?" local racer Bruce Tawson rhetorically asks. "You'd think the people would shut him down, but they haven't. The answer is, it's in his relationships. Somehow he keeps those relationships solid. He has a way of treating people well and assuring them and explaining what he's trying to accomplish."

Former NHRA employee Wayne McMurtry doesn't use the word "noise." Instead, he refers to unique sounds of drag racing that "the non-fan might find offensive" as "acoustical concerns."

"John has been able to work with the community," he observes. "He's a good neighbor and he's built a good neighbor policy. He's worked with all of the regulatory bodies to make it work. If John tells you he's going to do something, he does it. He'll make it happen."

Bandimere Jr.'s daughter Tami Shrader has learned a lot about dealing with these challenges from her father. In 1996, she founded an effective community outreach tool called Race To Read®. This six-week reading program for elementary students encourages literacy through race-themed incentives such as tickets to events at Bandimere Speedway. Since launching at Rooney Ranch Elementary School in Lakewood, the program has expanded to approximately 66 participating schools yearly throughout the greater Denver area.

"It has been a privilege to be involved with the town of Morrison," Shrader says. "We help hang their Christmas lights and we loan them tables and chairs for their seasonal events. And of course programs like Race To Read® really help strengthen that relationship. The support from the community for the racetrack is something the Bandimere family doesn't take for granted. We know we do something that makes noise, but we also recognize that most everyone has a need for speed at some point in life and we offer a safe, supervised place to enjoy going fast in an automobile or on a motorcycle off the city streets. It's more than just racing. It's about education and safety."

Dave Jackson is a local race enthusiast and for years has served as the Bandimere family's insurance provider. His daughter Erika participated in Race To Read® and the track's junior dragster program. Both had a significant impact.

"So many positive things have come out of that relationship with the Bandimere family and the track," Jackson says. "It's a family-run organization and they treat you like family. They include you. It's a really comfortable place to go and take your car and race and know that you're going to be safe. I'm in the insurance business so safety is kind of a big thing for me."

According to NHRA Division Five Director Rob Park, Bandimere Jr.'s proactive approach has not only created a bevy of ardent supporters who will fight for the track's life, he has also brought a certain level of class to a sport that traditionally hasn't always had the most favorable reputation.

"John is very involved in the community and the local Chambers of Commerce," he says. "John is philanthropic and heavily involved in the church. People on the outside of the sport might view drag racers as airheads and dirty under the fingernails and greasy. But he has changed the perception of motorsports in the Denver area by his presence."

The Bandimere's consistent commitment to its home city expands beyond Morrison and into all parts of Denver. One particularly noteworthy relationship can be found at Colorado Christian University where close family friend Dr. David Beckman who served on three occasions as president of Rockmont College (one of CCU's heritage institutions) and was instrumental in laying the groundwork for the university's steady growth. It was David Beckman's relationship with the family that caused John Sr. and Frances to name David Bandimere after this friend.

John Bandimere Sr. had a profound affect on Beckman as a teenager and John Bandimere Jr. spearheaded the creation of the Beckman Scholarship Annual Fund in honor of that relationship.

"The Bandimere family made a substantial contribution to get that scholarship started," CCU President Bill Armstrong says. "It's a fund where the money gets passed directly on to the students. Even to the very end of his life, a half century after he came to be the president at this university, he was still engaged here, and it gave him the utmost pleasure that a scholarship started by John Bandimere Sr.'s family in his name was helping students."

Armstrong often sees John and Lorraine Bandimere on campus at various sports activities and music and arts related events. During his tenure at CCU, he has appreciated the couple's unpretentious nature.

"Whenever there's something worthwhile going on in the community, they're always in the picture," Armstrong adds. "They're always there. They're always part of good things that are happening. They've had a cumulative effect over the years and impacted many lives."

Because of the family's relational approach to business, it has withstood multiple recessions, stock market instability and the ebb and flow of fan participation. Even in a mid-sized market such as Denver, Bandimere Speedway has somehow managed to keep its financial head above water.

"During the recession when everyone was going out of business and drag racing was losing its sponsors, John didn't lose one," Tawson says. "It's because he treats people well in good times and bad times. He's always talking to them and telling them his story. He's one of those unusual communicators in business who can keep people on his side no matter how bad the economy is."

In 2013, for instance, the Mopar Mile-High NHRA Nationals celebrated its 25th year in partnership with Mopar (Chrysler Corporation), the longest running title sponsorship in NHRA history.

"The Bandimere family has withstood challenges from construction and encroachment and the economy," Colorado Motorsports Hall of Fame president Rob Johnson says. "They continue to stand strong today. And they've done it without making enemies. They've treated people well. You look at how long Mopar has been a sponsor and that tells you everything you need to know about how they take care of people. That sets a great example of how it works when you do things the right way."

Eternal Returns

The last of the roughly 35,000 fans are filing out of Bandimere Speedway. The pit area, packed with roughly 400 race teams (depending on the class schedule any given year) is slowly evacuating as the crews load up their haulers and trailers. The cleanup crew is in full motion. Trash is being picked up. Concession stands are being inventoried. Merchandise is being boxed up for the next event.

Just a few minutes earlier, the coveted NHRA "Wally" trophies were handed out to champions in the professional categories of Top Fuel, Funny Car, Pro Stock and Pro Stock Motorcycle. Before that, the same coveted trophies were awarded to the sportsman champions. Perhaps most importantly, prize money was dispensed and valuable points were tallied as the teams continued to aim at the season-ending championship.

From a business standpoint, John Bandimere Jr. is well aware of the event's success. Tens of thousands of dollars have exchanged hands between the fans and various speedway representatives (i.e. ticket sellers, concession stand operators, merchandisers, etc.). But in this moment, Bandimere Jr. isn't thinking about those variables. Instead, his mind is consumed with one nagging thought.

"Did we make a difference in someone's life?"

No one should mistake his pensive contemplation for discontent. Bandimere Jr. is immensely thankful and grateful for everything the racetrack has provided he and his family. But as each year passes, he is less concerned about the financial bottom line and more gravely concerned about whether or not his family's investment into resources and relationships is yielding eternal returns.

In other words, is Bandimere Speedway serving as a platform from which the message of hope and life through a relationship with Jesus Christ can be plainly seen by anyone who comes in contact with the family or the racetrack?

It does matter to Bandimere Jr. that good friend Allen Johnson won his fifth Pro Stock title on Thunder Mountain. It matters more that Johnson took time that Sunday morning to gather with a couple hundred other drivers, crewmen and family members at the Racers For Christ chapel service.

That's why his thoughts often turn to people whose lives have been completely changed through their involvement at the track. Bandimere Jr. recalls special moments in time with men like Dave Howery and Dave Jackson and Mitch Mustard who accepted Christ as a result of God-ordained conversations. The entire Bandimere family thinks about the many members of the drag racing community that have yet to take that step, and it is their sincere desire to see more of them do so during their lifetime.

It's inevitable that at some point, Bandimere Jr. will catch a glimpse of that street sign in honor of his father that sits just to the east of the starting line. Bandimere Sr. has been gone for many years now, but his DNA (both physical and spiritual) lives on in the track and through the accomplishments of his children and grandchildren. It was through his father's example that Bandimere Jr. first understood what it meant to put people first and to genuinely care about their eternal wellbeing.

And that brings back to his memory Dr. David Beckman, the man for whom the Bandimere family spearheaded the Beckman Scholarship Annual Fund that benefits students at Colorado Christian University. Beckman went to be with the Lord four months before the 2014 Mopar Mile-High NHRA Nationals. His life was forever changed in the early 1940s through what seemed at the time to be a happenstance relationship with Bandimere Sr. and a small Sunday School class.

But Bandimere Jr. knows that there is no such thing as happenstance. His father always firmly believed the words found in Romans 8:28 and has learned to embrace them as well.

With that in mind, Bandimere Jr. mentally retraces steps from the previous three days. He measures his every word, his every action. He prays that at least one person saw something in him or his family or simply heard or felt something at the track that stood out and ultimately pointed them back to Christ.

"*That* is the Bandimere family's legacy," CCU President Bill Armstrong succinctly summarizes. "It's a legacy that is wrapped up in the example of what it means to live for Jesus Christ. It is the example of being a role model for men and women in everyday life and showing them what it looks like to have Jesus on your lips and in your heart. That is the greatest legacy that anyone can leave–to follow Jesus faithfully in good times or bad. *That* is the story of the Bandimere family."

Bandimere Speedway's Race-Themed Reading Program

Afterword

You just finished reading an amazing story of a family whose lives are tied together by the sport and business of drag racing. It is incredible to think that they have been racing cars on that hillside in Morrison, Colorado, for over 55 years. When you talk with the family and hear the stories, you find yourself laughing at one moment and moved to tears the next.

I will never forget my first introduction to John Bandimere Jr. He shared the story of the financial struggle the business faced when they rebuilt much of the facility. It was still a very emotional memory even though it had been close to twenty years since this took place. His tears were not from pain, however. No, the tears came from his understanding of the incredible blessing that had been bestowed upon them.

As you've read the book, I hope that you haven't missed the family's deeply held belief in Jesus Christ. Those tears in John's eyes also come from knowing that the Lord of Heaven and Earth reached out and provided for them in a way that they were unable of doing for themselves.

I have had the honor of watching the family live out their lives at the track. In doing that, it has become very apparent that they live out what they believe. So what is it that they believe? Do they really believe in the old stories of the Bible that tell of a God who loved the people of earth so much the he would send His Son to die for our wrongdoing?

For many people today that message of a God out there who loves them unconditionally is a tough thing to swallow. Let me share with you a story about a guy by the name of Saul who had the same problem. He had heard the message of this Son of God, but didn't buy into it. In fact he went out of his way to mistreat the people who did believe. One day Saul was traveling with friends when God spoke to him in a big way. There was no way he could continue to deny the existence and truth of Jesus. Within a few days he went from persecuting Christians to being a Christian himself.

One day Saul, now named Paul, was hanging out in the marketplace of a metropolitan city. Many intellectual and influential people routinely gathered there and discussed topics relevant to the day. Paul dropped in on a few of these discussions. He was very impressed with the sincerity of the different spiritual beliefs within the group. Finally, they asked him to join them and they gave him the chance to share what he believed. Here is what he said:

"The God who made the world and everything in it, this Master of sky and land, doesn't live in custom-made shrines or need the human race to run errands for him, as if he couldn't take care of himself. He makes the creatures; the creatures don't make him. Starting from scratch, he made the entire human race and made the earth hospitable, with plenty of time and space for living so we could seek after God, and not just grope around in the dark but actually find him. He doesn't play hide-and-seek with us. He's not remote; he's near. We live and move in him, can't get away from him! One of your poets said it well: 'We're the God-created.' Well, if we are the God-created, it doesn't make a lot of sense to think we could hire a sculptor to chisel a god out of stone for us, does it? "God overlooks it as long as you don't know any better—but that time is past. The unknown is now known, and he's calling for a radical life-change. He has set a day when the entire human race will be judged and everything set right. And he has already appointed the judge, confirming him before everyone by raising him from the dead." – Acts 17:24-31 (The Message)

Many people try to make the message of Jesus Christ really difficult to follow. They point to many roads and little paths that lead to unknown places. The people Paul was talking to in the story above were all looking for God. They just got lost on all the winding roads out there. While Jesus was alive on earth, He gave us a really good map. He said that He was going home to prepare rooms in the mansion for us. Someone asked the obvious question, "Where are you going and how do we get there?" Jesus laid out the road map for them.

"I am the way, the truth, and the life. No one can come to the father except through me." – John 14:6 (New Living Translation)

So there you go. Do you want to know how to reach out to God the Father? Jesus said to follow Him. No more wandering down those twisting roads or paths that lead to misery. No more searching for paths in the dark. He has prepared the way. Now you just need to reach out and have faith in Jesus.

The Bandimere family knows this path. You have seen from their story that it is not always smooth or without peril, but they continue to faithfully follow Jesus on the only path that leads to life with God. Will you reach out today and say yes to Jesus? Will you dive in and follow him on this path? – *Ken Webb, Bandimere Speedway Chaplain*

If you want to learn more about a relationship with Jesus Christ, visit:

www.bandimere.com/community/track-ministry-swm

The Historic Caddy Pickup

It is interesting how a vehicle is able to symbolize much of what a man and his family's lives are all about. The old "Caddy" Pickup is one of those strange objects that seemingly everyone in the family owns and yet no one seems to own. It seems to just have a life of it's own.

I was four years old when Mom and Dad took me with them to the old GMC truck lot in downtown Denver. In those days your choice in color was red, blue, black or green. Dad chose a blue one. I stood on the bench seat by Mom, mesmerized by all the colored trucks lined up in color sequence. It seemed forever before we finally left with the truck, but no surprise, Dad loved to talk and make friends.

It would be about 1951 or 1952 that he came up with the "forever" color scheme of two tone iridescent bronze and Montezuma gold with a white tonneau bed cover. My sister Joanna became quite popular when her high school friends would ride as a group in the back. Yes, there was a time when kids could ride in the back of a pick up without getting into trouble.

In 1955 Dad would be told about a new Cadillac commercial funeral hearse to be found in Cheyenne, Wyoming that had been burned by vandals. He engineered a way to adapt his '49 GMC body to his new acquisition, a commercial Cadillac frame, running gear and amenities. He wanted a show truck that was practical and rugged with the Cadillac feel. He ended up with one of the first custom vehicles to be on Denver streets, that also was a great street racer.

The truck was first photographed and debuted at the 1955 first NHRA event in Great Bend, Kansas. It was sporting its real Cadillac wire wheels.

John Sr., John Jr. and David would drive it to Los Angeles to pick up the Cummins diesel Indy race car. On the way to LA we stopped for the night off the highway. It was very dark and Dad prepared a place to sleep in the bed of the truck the best way he could. In the middle of the night we about jumped out of our skins as a train passed by. We did not know we were literally right next to the tracks.

It would be a short time later that John Sr. and John Jr. would go to Detroit to show it off and street race Detroit style. On the way to Detroit Dad is sleeping with John Jr. at the wheel, when John Jr. goes to sleep as well. As the truck starts to take out a row of 6 x 6 wood road makers, Dad awakens in time to grab the wheel and avoid total disaster. Needless to say the show and tell time in Detroit was not quite as spectacular.

After repairs the truck was the tow vehicle for many race venues. The folks and I took it to the Salt Flats on several occasions, towing the Plymouth race cars, and two complete engines in the back. Wow, what a truck and what a ride!

In 1964 we found a wrecked 1961 Cadillac with 8000 miles. Frank Peterson, Dad and I worked many late nights to convert the running gear, steering and other amenities to the truck. Frank hand made some new beautiful styled bumpers, which set off the truck. Lou Senter of Ansen Enterprises equipped us with four new aluminum dish wheels and two more for the twin side mounts. The big surprise came when Dad said I could take it to Los Angeles to school at Biola University. He rode with Mom and I to Colorado Springs to make sure the truck was doing okay and Dad caught a bus back to Denver. Mom and I would take our last trip together before her death. My future wife Barbara soon met my Mom at the school dorm in the truck with me. This was their one and only meeting.

I had great times showing off that truck around LA, street racing and cruising. As I cruised down Sunset Strip I realized this pick up was made for Hollywood.

Barb and I had our first date in the pick up going to Knott's Berry Farm for the Biola University school year kick off. The joy of having chrome running boards was for me to pick her up and put her in her seat so she would not step on them.

Before the school year was over I put the fan into the radiator when the water pump to fan shaft broke. John Jr. flew out and helped me repair it and we drove it back to Denver. We stopped in Idaho Springs for breakfast to hear of the awful Platte River flood that hit Denver that day.

From that time until the early '80's this would be Dad's work truck and his last street racer.

In 1986 the Sabers of Denver Car Club dedicated their annual car show at the Currigan Convention Center to Dad. I dug the truck out of "moth balls," got it to look as good as I could for the show and for Dad's honor. A short time later he passed away. Having the truck at the Saber Show would be his last ride.

In 1995 we were asked to bring it to the 40th Reunion of the Great Bend, Kansas NHRA event. We found out it was one of only a handful of vehicles still in existence from the 1955 event.

A dear friend loaned me a dually and an enclosed trailer. We cleaned it up as best we could and made the event. While at the old Great Bend track site, I ran into Mr. Leslie Lovett, the Peterson Publishing photographer, who shot the 1955 event. He re-shot pictures of the truck right where it had sat 40 years prior.

It has been in storage until 2010. Since then I have been doing a full frame off restoration. We are bringing her up to date with newer Cadillac amenities. "She" will look the same but ride much better very soon. It will be grand to have the "old girl" back on Denver streets. – *David Bandimere*